Festivals
for You to Celebrate

By Susan Purdy

HOLIDAY CARDS FOR YOU TO MAKE

IF YOU HAVE A YELLOW LION

CHRISTMAS DECORATIONS FOR YOU TO MAKE

MY LITTLE CABBAGE

FESTIVALS
FOR YOU TO
CELEBRATE

SUSAN PURDY

J. B. LIPPINCOTT COMPANY

Philadelphia

For Miss V. Louise Higgins
Teacher and inspiration extraordinaire

Acknowledgments

For information and invaluable assistance in the research and preparation of this book, the author wishes to express her indebtedness and gratitude to all who helped including the following individuals and institutions: Charley and Andreas Kanas, Mrs. Robin G. Wilder, Mr. and Mrs. Gabor Peterdi, Miss Katherine Dezsenyi, Mrs. Norma Bredbury, Mrs. Doris Jason, Mrs. Lucy Jampoler, Mr. W. I. Art, Mr. Szu Heng Loh, Mr. Mark Pivavonski, Mr. Geoffrey Steinfeld, Mrs. Irene Nugent, my sister Nancy Gold, and most important, my husband Geoffrey Purdy; also the Official Belgian Tourist Bureau; British Travel Association; Danish Information Office; Nathan Freedman, Director of Public Relations, Israel Government Tourist Office; Mr. J. Hobden and Miss Jean Masters, Westfield C. P. School, Westfield, England; Greek National Tourist Office; Swiss National Tourist Office; Mrs. Hanna, Cepelia Corporation; Embassy of India Information Service; Embassy of Iran, Office of Press and Information; Israel Information Services; Istituto Italiano di Cultura; Italian State Tourist Office; Rudolf F. Mattesich, U. S. Representative, Austrian State Tourist Department; Mexican National Tourist Council; Norwegian Information Service; Toru Ohkata, Japan National Tourist Organization; Casa de Portugal, Portuguese Information, Tourist and Trade Office; Signora Raspini, Direttrice Didattica, Scuola Regina Elena, Rome; Spanish National Tourist Office; Swedish Information Service; Mario Labastida del Valle, Mexican Government Tourism Department; and the Venezuelan Consulate; and Mrs. Julie Goss.

For reading the manuscript and offering valuable criticism and advice, the author wishes to thank Rabbi Samuel Schwartz, the Reverend Robert L. Green, Jr., and the Very Reverend Joseph F. Cleary, J.C.D. However, the author accepts full responsibility for any discrepancies or errors in the material.

Table of Contents

(9)

 **Introduction**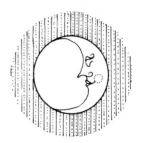

Since the earth's first men noticed the seasonal changes of the sun, moon, stars, and weather, they celebrated these miraculous occurrences with awe and reverence. Early man did not understand that the spring would automatically return each year; he believed the warm sun would follow winter only if magical rites were performed in its honor. So, too, were rituals required to bring rain for crops, to honor the shortest and longest days of the year (winter and summer solstices) and the beginning of spring and fall (vernal or spring equinox, and autumnal or fall equinox), to make snow disappear, to welcome spring plants, to cure disease, and to thank the mysterious forces of nature for the harvest.

Through the centuries, men learned more about themselves and the natural sciences. Religions developed, offered explanations for many of the mysteries and transformed many of the old rituals to its own purposes. Science provided its own answers. But knowledge did not prevent men from continuing to observe the ancient rituals. These varied from one country to another, but the basic response—holidays and festivals—was the same. While more of nature's phenomena are understood today, festivals are loved no less; though some have been changed or forgotten, many of the oldest are still preserved. In addition, many new holidays—patriotic, national, international, and local—have been created. Despite changes in calendars, politics, and history, holidays remain, adapting but never quite disappearing.

A study of holidays becomes a study of humanity, for all men are united in the sharing of common seasonal festivals. At the same time, the infinite variety in the manner of celebrating displays the individual personality of each country and its people. This can be clearly seen in the craft projects, of authentic national origin, included in this book. Excluding patriotic festivals, the holidays described are those most widely observed in the United States. They are traced from their origins to their present-day celebrations, and wherever possible, similar festivals of other countries have been included for comparison and contrast, providing a fuller understanding of holidays around the world. Upon the framework of the year's seasons, the essential oneness of all men, their distinct national personalities, and their religious differences and similarities are woven together into the rich and colorful fabric of the world's festivals.

How to Use This Book

FESTIVALS is designed to be used by groups as well as by individuals. There is wide variety among the craft activities included. Some are easy and quick to make, others are more complex and time consuming. Young people between the ages of eight and eighty will find challenging and unusual activities to fit their abilities. It is hoped that this book, and specifically the Activities Subject Index, page 186, will be used as a reference source from which to draw fresh ideas and inspiration in the celebration of festival *and* ordinary days.

Most of the material may be adapted to fit any occasion. The costumes and masks included may be used at any type of costume party; favors, decorations, special foods, and games may brighten a Bon Voyage, Welcome Home, Mother's or Father's Day, or Birthday party as well as a school pageant or fair. Designs and decorations may be simplified or elaborated upon depending on one's individual talents. By drawing freely from all the craft and text materials, you will find yourself creating vastly enriched and individualized holiday celebrations.

The following suggestions are offered as a guide to the planning of group celebrations. Before final planning, project directions should be read through and consideration given to such elements as materials needed, project's relative complexity, and length of time required. The latter is not always indicated, as it depends upon such variables as manual dexterity, talent, working conditions, attention span, etc.

HALLOWEEN, CARNIVAL, MARDI GRAS

For your Halloween, Carnival, or Mardi Gras party or festival, a bazaar or fair may be organized with booths featuring various activities chosen from the Activities Subject Index, page 186. For example, a Games of Skill booth might include the *Flower Toss, Knocking of the Eggs,* and *Jump the Flame.* A Fortune-Telling booth might have a costumed gypsy presiding over such activities as *Wax Fortunes, Apple Peel Fortunes,* and *Alphabet Charms.* An International Holiday Foods booth might serve, or sell *Austrian Marzipan, Scottish Hogmanay*

Shortbread, or *Swedish Vanilla Cookies*. A Mask-Making booth might provide materials for making either *Paper Bag* or *Tinfoil Masks*. Prizes may be given to the winners of races (*Pancake Race*, *Walnut Boat Race*, *Flaming Wheel Contest*) and to the most original entries in a costume parade (*Costumes and Masks*). Apples may be bobbed for in tubs of water or hanging from a stick (*Balancing Apple*). Floats may be made in the manner of Mardi Gras, with costumed characters representing different holidays in different countries.

THANKSGIVING

A Thanksgiving festival might include an adaptation of the traditional history of the American holiday—in play, verse, or speech form—as well as a presentation of the harvest holidays of other peoples and other countries. All presentations should include demonstrations of appropriate activities or samples of craft projects. For example, one small group might make a *Kern Maiden* and explain her origin, while another group might make and display *Turnip Lanterns* and *Jack-o'-Lanterns*, discussing their origin and similarity. *Turkey Mobiles*, Indian *Alpana Designs*, and Mexican *Ojo de Dios* may be made by the entire group as decorations for the room or stage, and their significance explained. *Fruit Animals* may be made as table centerpieces, and the Jewish holiday of Succot described. The entire group might, in addition, wish to follow the English custom of *Harvest Home*, gathering foods, fruits, and flowers in baskets and distributing them to needy families, thus sharing the meaning of Thanksgiving.

MIDWINTER FESTIVAL

A Midwinter Festival or pageant might be International and Interfaith, including selected elements from the chapters on St. Lucia Day, St. Nicholas Day, Christmas, Chanukah, Epiphany, New Year, and Rosh Hashanah. Or, each holiday might be the subject of a separate presentation, as described below.

CHRISTMAS AND CHANUKAH

A Christmas pageant might begin with a presentation based upon St. Lucia Day in which young girls, dressed in Lucia costumes and displaying the traditionally shaped *Lucia Rolls* or cookies, describe the meaning of their Scandinavian holiday. In addition, one might hold a Lucia Beauty Contest. St. Nicholas Day follows, with a group of boys wearing the Swiss *St. Nicholas Headdresses* they have made. Other boys are dressed as Bishop Nicholas and his helper, Black Pete. In turn, they explain who they are and tell the story of St. Nicholas. In addition, there might be a costumed American Santa Claus to tell the story of *his* origin. Other members of the group might describe the meaning and history of the various Christmas symbols while displaying objects they have made of these symbols, such as *Holly Place Card*, *Mistletoe Holder*, *Advent Wreath*, etc. A prominently displayed Christmas Tree whose origin should be explained, may be trimmed with decorations of different countries (*Austrian Covered Nuts*, *Hawaiian Kinipopo*, *Swedish Julehjerter*, etc.). After the festival, the decorated tree might be donated to a hospital or children's home. The Jewish holiday of Chanukah may be described, and the traditional *Dreidle Games* played by a few members of the group.

For a gay finale, a Mexican Christmas *Piñata* party might include the entire group, with piñata gifts or candies for all.

EPIPHANY

An Epiphany festival might open with a presentation of the scene at Christ's birth: the Holy Family gathered about the manger, surrounded by costumed angels, and the *Three Kings*, who describe to the audience the origin of the holiday. The Italian festival of the Befana may follow, with the Befana's legend acted out in play form with puppets (*Eggshell Puppet*) or dolls (*Befana Doll*). Or, the legend may simply be recounted while *Befana Dolls*, made by the speakers, are displayed.

As in France and England, the *Epiphany Bean Cake* might be the focal point of an Epiphany party, in which prizes and a gilded *Crown* are given to the King and Queen of the Bean. The *Twelve Days of Christmas Mobile*, made at the start of the holiday season, may be taken apart at this time and the small gifts inside the boxes distributed.

NEW YEAR

A New Year's party might be highlighted by culinary specialties from many different countries. In addition to offering such New Year foods as *Scottish*

Hogmanay Shortbread, Austrian Marzipan, and *English Wassail,* a *First Footer* might be featured to tell the guests' fortunes. *Janus Pins* might either be favors given to all guests, or reserved as special door prizes.

A small group might enjoy a New Year *Marzipan* party, in which the principal activity is the making of marzipan fruits and animals, which might then be given as gifts.

A New Year's pageant might present members of the group explaining the New Year customs of various countries while displaying their crafts. For example, *Dragon Lanterns* may be shown while relating the story of the Chinese New Year; *Sabzeh* seedlings may be displayed, then poured out into a pan of water while describing the traditions of the Iranian New Year, and *Apple and Honey* may be exhibited as symbols of the Jewish New Year, Rosh Hashanah.

VALENTINE'S DAY

At a Valentine's Day party, various types of cards may be made and/or exchanged. Refreshments might consist of decorated Hungarian *Mézeskalács* cookies, and for activities, *Welsh Love Spoons* or *Tussie Mussies* may be made and love fortunes told (*Wax Fortunes, Apple Peel Fortune,* and *Alphabet Charm*) while the history of the day is related.

SPRING AND SUMMER

Spring or Summer Festivals or pageants might include groups presenting the celebrations of different countries, illustrated with craft articles, games, etc. For example, one unit might display their *Carp Kites* while telling of Tango-no-Sekku in Japan; another group might stage a May Day celebration complete with *Flora Dolls, Maypoles,* and *Flower Toss* games.

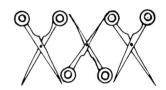 **Materials**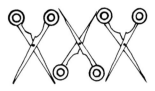

The following is a list of all the materials mentioned in this book, although each project will require the use of ony a few items at a time. Materials can easily be found in your home, local stationery store, 5 & 10 cent store, art supply or craft shop, or hardware store. If you have any trouble finding materials, look in the yellow pages of the telephone book. Use the materials suggested or make up your own variations.

NOTE: Throughout this book, the symbol " has been used for inches, and ′ for feet. Before beginning any project, read all the directions through to the end. Read the instructions on tracing and transferring patterns on Page 18.

ruler, tape measure
pencil, colored pencils, crayons
pen, colored felt or nylon-tipped pens (oil and water base)
scissors (regular shears), small manicure scissors, pinking shears (optional)
stapler
exacto knife, small paring knife, grapefruit knife (optional), kitchen knife
paper clips, paper clamps (cross-shaped paper clips)
masking and cellophane tape
apron
rubber cement, Elmer's or Sobo glue
white facial tissues, absorbent cotton (puffs or roll)
newspapers
cotton swab sticks or lollypop sticks
paper towels
wax paper
cup hook
ribbon, braided straw ribbon (optional), raffia
wool (medium-thick, bright colors)
string (medium-thick, cotton, white and red)
pipe cleaners (white and colored)
wire #32 "thread" wire; stiff, but flexible wire, such as #12 copper wire or
    wire clothes hanger, for mobile
wire cutters

(15)

styrofoam ball (1″ or 2″ diameter)
straight pins, map pins, corsage pins (optional)
pin backs (to glue on back of decorative pins, found in craft shops)
darning needle, fine sewing needle
nails (with heads)
hammer
thumbtacks
toothpicks (wood and plastic)
tweezers
tin cans (one open end)
wooden dowels or sticks (about ¼″ diameter)
spatula
cookie sheets
large mixing bowl, tin or glass pie-plate, small bowls or cups
mixing spoon, measuring spoons, and measuring cup
leaves and branches (evergreen *and* non-evergreen)
coconut palm fronds (optional)
pine cone
mistletoe
white cotton cloth (old sheet or unbleached muslin)
feathers (assorted colors and sizes)
flashlight
orange balloons
"Hula" hoop, smooth barrel hoop or cardboard barrel top with flat surface
  removed
sand or dirt (in foil-lined box)
paper milk carton (one quart size, empty)
tinfoil (silver or gold)
stiff colored foil
construction paper, glazed or origami paper, crepe paper, tissue paper
colored cellophane
desk blotters or cheesecloth
brown paper bags (#10 or #12), large clear plastic bags
cardboard, shirt cardboards, bristol board (1- or 2-ply) or stiff poster paper,
  heavy mat board or corrugated cardboard, oaktag
cardboard tubes (from paper towel of wax paper rolls)
cardboard boxes (shirt-size), cigar box (sometimes given away by drugstores)
tempera paint or water colors (water base and washable)
powdered poster paint
paint brushes, small new brushes for decorating candies

(16)

Easter egg dyes
vegetable food coloring
white shellac
alcohol (solvent for washing shellac brush)
self-hardening clay (found in art supply stores, does not require firing)
plasticene clay
plaster of paris (found in art supply or hardware stores)
art gum ("soap") erasers, 1" by 2", or 2" by 3" size (large size found in art
    supply stores)
paraffin wax, double boiler to melt wax
old candle stubs, red birthday candles or red "flower tapers"
block printing tool
vegetable peeler
can opener (V-ended, puncture type)
small tin bells

FOODS

almond extract, almond paste
almonds, whole blanched
birdseed
butter or margarine
candy (stick candy, chocolate shots, marshmallows)
corn (ear with husks on)
eggs
flour, rice flour (optional)
fruits, assorted whole (apples, lemons, oranges, etc.)
ginger ale
ice cream
juices
nuts, assorted whole (pecans, almonds, walnuts, etc.)
onions (yellow and Spanish red)
saffron (dry stigmas of a variety of crocus plant, used as yellow dye and food
    seasoning, found in food store)
suet
sugar, confectioners', granulated
turnips, yellow
vanilla extract
vegetable food dye
vinegar

(17)

How to Trace and Transfer Patterns

Always trace patterns, *never* cut book, or you will destroy the directions on the other side of the page, and will not have the patterns to reuse year after year. *Note:* Throughout the book, the symbol " has been used for inches, and ' for feet.

1. Place a piece of tracing paper over the whole pattern you want to copy. Pull edges of tracing paper over book and tape them to table to hold drawing steady.

2. With pencil, lightly trace pattern outline onto tracing paper. (If you press too hard, you will tear through tracing and into book). Also trace dotted lines, which mean *fold,* and all other markings *within* pattern.

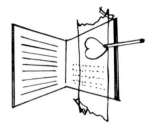

3. Lift tracing off book and place it *face down* on scrap paper. With soft, dark pencil, rub all over *back* of tracing (a). To transfer onto dark colored paper, rub with white chalk instead of pencil. *Note:* Instead of scribbling on back of tracing, you can place a sheet of carbon paper, *black side down,* between tracing and paper, and draw over it to transfer pattern (b).

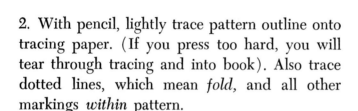

4. Compare transferred pattern to original in book to be sure that you have traced all lines. Pattern is now ready to be cut out.

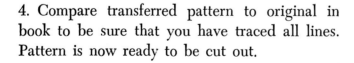

How to Knot Thread

1. Wind end of thread two or three times around tip of index finger.

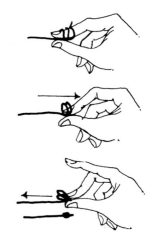

2. Pull index finger back from tip of thumb as shown, pressing finger against thumb and rolling thread to very end of index finger.

3. Bring tip of middle finger down to hold rolled thread while, with the other hand, you pull (arrow) on length of thread, tightening roll and making knot.

How to Score Paper

To make a neat fold in a stiff piece of paper, the surface of the paper may be scored, or lightly cut, with a sharp knife. Scoring is not necessary for soft paper such as construction paper that folds easily. *Note:* SCORING IS DONE WITH A SHARP KNIFE, OR EXACTO KNIFE, AND THEREFORE CAN BE DANGEROUS. DO NOT USE KNIFE WITHOUT PERMISSION OR ADULT SUPERVISION.

To Score a Line:

1. Before scoring, decide in which direction you will want fold to close. The scored edge should be on the *outside*. Place paper on table *outside surface up*.

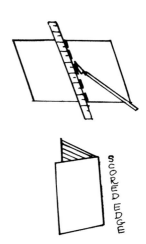

2. Hold ruler against dotted "fold" line to be scored. Run knife along ruler's edge very lightly, with one stroke, cutting only surface of paper, slightly deeper than a scratch. DO NOT CUT THROUGH PAPER.

3. Now fold paper along scored line, keeping cut surface on *outside* of fold. Press fold flat.

(19)

How to Cut Squares and Circles

SQUARES

Method I—Used when paper may not be folded.

1. Determine desired length of square sides (4″ in example). On two cut edges of rectangular paper, measure and mark off points 4″ from *one* corner, as shown.

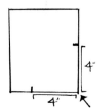

2. Measure and mark off a third point, 4″ in from right point and 4″ above bottom point. With ruler, draw lines connecting points. Cut out square.

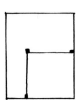

Method II—Used when paper may be folded without harming design.

1. To cut square from rectangular paper, fold edge A down even with edge B. Press diagonal fold flat.

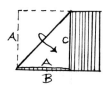

2. Holding edges A and B together firmly, cut along edge C. Discard strip and unfold square paper.

CIRCLES

Method I—Used when paper may not be folded.

1. On *square* paper, measure and mark off half-way point on each side.
2. To draw circle, sketch arcs connecting each point. Cut out.

(20)

Method II—Used when paper may be folded without harming design.

1. Fold rectangular paper in half, then in half again, as shown.

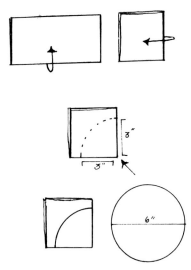

2. To make a circle 6″ across, measure and mark off points 3″ from bottom right corner (arrow). *Note:* the "radius," or distance from center of circle to edge, is one half the "diameter," or total distance across circle.

3. Draw a curved line connecting points. Cut along this line. Unfold circle.

Method III—Easiest method, if you have a compass or two pencils and some string.

1. Set compass legs at desired circle radius (3″ for a 6″ circle). Set point of compass in center of paper and swing pencil around, drawing circle. Cut out.

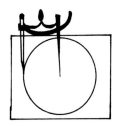

2. The same effect may be had using two pencils and some string. Tie a piece of string between two pencil tops as shown, the distance between pencils equal to radius of circle (3″). *Keeping both pencils exactly perpendicular to paper,* hold the point of one in paper's center and swing the other around, drawing circle. Cut out.

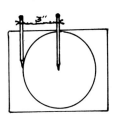

AUTUMN

The autumnal equinox, one of the two days of the year when the sun crosses the celestial equator, has since earliest history been observed as a special day, ushering in the autumn season. Depending upon where in the world one lives, or which calendar one uses, autumn may be a time of endings, beginnings, or joyful celebrations.

To some, autumn means the end of summer's warmth and pleasures, but it brings instead brilliantly colored falling leaves, Halloween, harvests, and thanksgiving. To others, it is also the time for welcoming the New Year.

Halloween

Our name for this holiday comes from the Christian Church, which celebrates its holiday, All Hallow's Eve, at the same time. Actually, Halloween is an ancient, pre-Christian celebration which originated with the Druids who lived centuries ago in the lands that are now the British Isles and France. Druids worshipped the natural and supernatural worlds, and used a Celtic calendar in which October 31 was the last day of the year, their New Year's Eve. On this day, they held an autumn festival called Samhain, which marked the beginning of winter and honored Saman, Lord of Death. He allowed witches, demons, ghosts, and other spirits to wander about freely for the night, and in the hope of influencing these frightening creatures, the Druids recited special chants, lit bonfires, and made offerings of sweets and special foods. Most important, they disguised themselves in masks and costumes so the spirits would not recognize them and thus could do them no harm. It is possible to see many of our own Halloween traditions in these early Druidic rites.

When the Christian religion began to grow, it often adapted pagan holidays to its own purposes. Thus, the Samhain festival of the Druids was given the name All Hallow's Eve, the night before All Hallow's Day, or All Saints' Day, November 1, when one honored the "all hallowed" saints of the church who did not have their own festival days during the year.

Most of the superstitions and customs associated with Halloween in America had their origin in the British Isles and Ireland. For example, there are many explanations for the tradition of trick-or-treating, but it seems most logically to have originated in Ireland, where legend tells that the custom began with the farmers who, centuries ago, went from house to house in their villages asking for food for their Halloween festivities in the name of the ancient god *Muck Olla*. They promised good luck and wealth to the givers and threatened the stingy with bad luck and the god's wrath. It is also possible that trick-or-treating began with the poor who went begging for All Souls' Cake on All Souls' Day. Children later copied this custom, and continue in England to go from house to house asking for treats. They often dress up, sometimes boys and girls switch clothes and don masks, carrying on the ancient belief that evil spirits cannot recognize and thus cannot hurt one who is disguised. Since the days of the Druids, masks have been an important part of one's costume for this reason. Their variety is unlimited, and they can be made out of practically any material. The following masks may be made simply and quickly in any style.

(23)

PAPER-BAG MASKS

Materials: Paper bags, size #10 or #12 (bag must be big enough to fit like a hat on top of head, but not necessarily over whole head), colored felt pens or crayons, pencil, scissors, stapler, cotton string.

1. a. Open bag, bottom up; bottom now becomes *top* of hat.

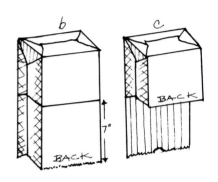

   b. On back and two sides, draw line around bag as shown, about 7″ up from open end. *Note:* Front panel (face mask) remains full length.

   c. On either side of front panel, cut up sides about 7″. Then cut around marked line, removing 7″ strip of back and sides.

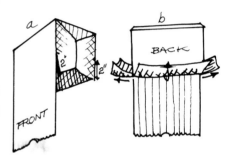

2. Cut 2″ up each side of back and front panels (a). Fold up these 2″ flaps on back and sides as shown (b).

3. With flaps folded up, staple each side twice, about ¼″ up from folded edge (a). Then fold flaps down along stapled line, making hat brim (b).

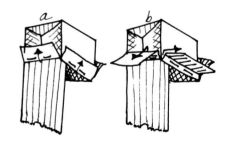

4. To make hat brim on front panel, fold up a 1″ deep flap at point even with side flaps (a). Staple this flap across front, placing staples along fold (b).

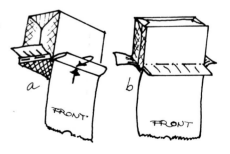

5. To make feather, draw shape as shown on top of hat (a). *Leaving base of feather attached*

(24)

to bag, cut around its outline. Fold up feather, as shown (b).

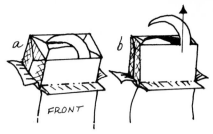

6. Draw face on front panel beneath brim. Draw hat band just above brim on sides, back and front. Decorate feather (or staple real feather to it). *Note:* Felt pen ink bleeds through paper bags. Place bags on newspaper when decorating.

7. When designs are dry, fold up brim flaps on each side. With scissors or pencil point, make two small holes, just beneath staple line, in center of each side (a). Pull cotton string (about 16″ long) through holes, tie one end to itself on the inside, leave one end at least 14″ long. Repeat on opposite side (b). These strings tie under your chin.

8. With scissors or pencil point, make two small holes on either side of face panel as shown. Pull string through holes, tie one end to itself on the inside, and leave one end of each string at least 14″ long. These strings hold face mask in place and tie in back of your head.

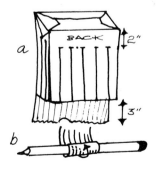

KING OR QUEEN BAG-MASK VARIATIONS

1. In step 1—a, b, and c (left), cut away only a 3″ strip from bottom of back and sides of bag.

2. On each side of front and back panels, cut straight up to within 2″ of top. On these side and back panels, cut wide strips (for curls) up to within 2″ from hat top (a). Roll each curl up over pencil, as shown (b).

(25)

3. In step 5 (page 24) cut away entire flat top of hat (original bottom of bag) (a). Cut top edge of hat into crown pattern such as suggested (b) or of your own design.

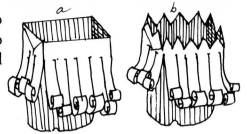

4. Decorate face and crown as in step 6 (page 26) Add side strings as in step 7, *except,* make holes for strings in the 2″ crown above the side curls. Add face strings as in step 8.

NOTE: At a Halloween party, divide guests into pairs or teams. Give each pair, or each team, paper bags and necessary art materials to make masks. Set time limit, give prize to whichever individual or team finishes mask-making first. Grand prizes may be given for funniest, prettiest, or most imaginative mask.

TINFOIL MASK

Materials: Tinfoil, oil-base felt pens, cotton string, scissors.

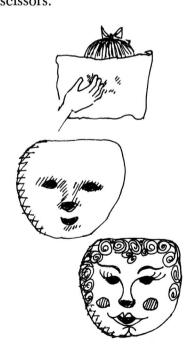

1. Cut an 8″ square of tinfoil (see page 20, method I). Press foil over your face, pushing it against facial contours to shape nose, cheeks, eyes, chin.

2. Remove foil from face. *Do not flatten.* Fold square edges toward the underside, making outer shape of mask roughly fitted to face.

3. *With foil mask on table,* cut eye and nose holes. Cut mouth hole if desired.

4. With oil-base felt pens, decorate mask face.

(26)

5. With point of scissors, make a hole ½″ in from each side of face (X's).

6. Cut two strings, 16″ long. Pull one through each hole, tie it to itself over mask's edge. Keep knot on inside. Let long string hang down on each side, to be tied behind head.

The jack-o'-lantern also had an Irish origin. According to the legend, there once was a fellow named Jack who was so stingy, and who had played so many practical jokes, that he was forbidden from entering either heaven or hell when he died. Instead, he was condemned forever to wander the earth with his lantern. On Halloween night, you can sometimes see him passing by. The English and Irish in America discovered that the pumpkin made a very good jack-o'-lantern, though before they had often used winter squash and turnips (see page 49). The pumpkin has become one of Halloween's most popular symbols. Following are some jack-o'-lantern ideas for your Halloween party.

PUMPKIN BALLOON

This balloon may be a Halloween party invitation or a gay decoration.

Material: Orange balloons (jumbo size, about 9″ by 5″ when deflated), black oil-base felt pen.

1. Place balloon flat on table. With felt pen, write greeting, invitation, or draw designs or jack-o'-lantern face. Let one side dry before turning over balloon to decorate other side. *Note:* If you are using a smaller size balloon, blow it up (*pinch end closed,* do not tie or knot) and decorate, holding until ink dries. Deflate to mail as invitation.

(27)

2. When ink on jumbo balloon is dry, blow up balloon and pinch end closed (do not tie or knot) while examining design. Design may be touched up while inflated. Place balloon in envelope to mail as invitation, or hang balloon jack-o'-lanterns around the room for your Halloween party.

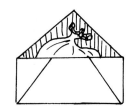

JACK-O'-LANTERN FRUIT CUP

Materials: Oranges, canned fruit cup or assorted fresh fruits (bananas, strawberries, pineapples, cherries, peaches, etc.), paring knife, grapefruit knife (optional), mixing bowl, spoon, paper towel, toothpicks (colored if possible), vegetable food coloring (blue or green).

1. Wash orange. Cut top off as shown.

2. Using grapefruit or paring knife, cut out orange sections and scoop out inside of shell with spoon, leaving peel whole. Save orange thus removed.

3. To prepare fruit cup, cut orange sections into small pieces; wash, peel and cut fresh fruit into small pieces. Or, open can of fruit cup (assorted fruits packed in syrup). Combine all fruit in bowl.

4. Rinse, then dry outside of scooped-out orange with paper towel. Using toothpick or paring knife point, scratch jack-o'-lantern face into orange as shown. Also scratch "ribs" on orange top, and insert half toothpick in center for stem.

5. Drip blue or green food coloring into scratched lines, staining them. Wipe off excess coloring with paper towel.

6. When face is dry, spoon fruit mixture into orange. Set jack-o'-lantern on dish, cover fruit with cap, and serve. (May be chilled first in refrigerator.) For a Halloween party, make an orange jack-o'-lantern for each guest.

Superstition and magic, often involving plants and animals, have been part of the Halloween celebration since the Druids, who held cats sacred, their cat form being punishment for evildoing. Many years after the Druids, when witchcraft became popular in Europe, it was believed that witches took the form of cats. For this reason, we today associate black cats with Halloween witches. Since this is the season when spirits roam freely, it is an especially effective time for us, as it was for witches or Druids, to use charms of love and fortune.

WAX FORTUNES

Pouring hot lead or wax through a wedding ring into cold water is an ancient fortune-telling custom popular in many parts of the world. Lead is too dangerous to use; the following method uses paraffin wax. *Note:* As the use of a stove and the handling of hot wax is required, this project should be done only with the help of an adult. Remember, paraffin is flammable if overheated or exposed to open flame; use only a double boiler to melt wax.

Materials: Paraffin wax (or old candle stubs), double boiler (or clean tin can set in partially filled pan of water), bucket or bowl of cold water, spoon or ladle.

1. Melt wax in double boiler, over low heat. (Read caution note above.)

2. When wax is melted, remove it from heat. Set top of double boiler containing wax on dish or hot plate. Each participant, in turn, should ladle or spoon a small amount of hot wax from pot and drip it into bowl of cold water.

3. Read your fortunes in the shapes formed by the cooled wax. For example: a rectangle might mean "suitcase, going on a trip"; circle—"money"; teardrop—"sadness"; letter of alphabet—"true love's initial"; flower shape—"love." *Note:* At a costume Halloween party, a gypsy could read wax fortunes for the other guests.

ALPHABET CHARM

Originally, a crystal goblet and a gold wedding band were required for this English fortune-telling custom. However, a drinking glass and an ordinary ring will divine just as effectively.

Materials: Drinking glass, masking tape, carpet thread or fine string, ring.

1. Press band of tape across top of glass just to one side of center, as shown.

2. Cut piece of thread slightly longer than height of glass. Tie one end of thread around ring. Hang ring down in center of glass, not quite touching bottom, and tape other end of thread to center of cross band.

3. To discover the name of your sweetheart, hold glass in one hand, raised above your head. Close your eyes, and recite the alphabet aloud very slowly. Every time the ring strikes the side of the glass, stop, put down the glass, and write down the letter you were at when ring struck. Or, if in a group, a second player can write letters for you. After recording letter, raise glass, start reciting again. This method will eventually give you either your sweetheart's initials or name.

FIVE GRAINS FORTUNE

This old English custom originally used five sheaves of grain, which were placed on a barn floor. Each sheaf was given a name: "wishes," "wealth," "happiness," "work," and "sorrow." A sleepy hen was brought from the hen-house and encouraged to walk about in the grain; whichever sheaf she finally chose to peck at determined one's fortune. Here is a modern version, for telling the fortunes of a group.

Materials: Five paper bags, crayons, colored pencils or felt pens, string or ribbon to tie bags, miniature favors (bought or made yourself—see step 2 below), blindfold (handkerchief).

1. Each bag is named for a fortune: sorrow, wealth, happiness, work, wishes. Decorate outside of bags with appropriate symbols and label.

2. Fill each container with favors related (in serious or ridiculous manner) to each type of fortune. For example: *sorrow*—broom, shovel, teardrops, handkerchief; *wealth*—coins or candy money, list of poor friends to remember, money bag, piggy bank; *happiness*—ring, letter, paper flower, paper sun, suitcase, candy; *work*—toy car, truck or plane, hammer, nail, spool of thread, pencil, toy guitar, crayon, musical notes; *wishes* —toy plane, paper palm tree, boat, skates, ball, candy, etc.

3. Fill bags, tie them closed, and place them on floor or table. Guests stand around them in circle. One player at a time is blindfolded; bags are shuffled, and player is spun around several times in place before being allowed to pick a bag. This choice determines his fortune. Blindfold is removed, bag is opened, and player must, *without looking inside,* pick out one favor and describe to group how he will use it.

The ancient Romans had a celebration on November 1 in honor of Pomona, the goddess of orchards and gardens. The festivities included the eating of apples, which were the special fruit of the day. At one time, Europe and the British Isles were part of the vast Roman Empire and the people of these countries eventually adopted the Roman traditions. Thus, the Roman love of apples became part of the European, and finally American, celebration of Halloween. Two of the oldest apple customs are bobbing for apples that hang on strings or float on water. More unusual is the following game adapted from an old English custom of balancing a lit candle on one end of a sword and a bobbing apple on the other. The idea was to bite the apple without getting burned.

BALANCING APPLE

Materials: One flat wooden stick about 2′ long, cotton string, 2 paper cups, thumbtacks, apple with stem, water or paper confetti or rice.

1. Cut piece of string 18″ long. Tie one end of string to apple stem, the other end loosely around one end of stick. *Note:* Final knot will be made after stick is balanced. Apple is to hang down from stick so it will be mouth height when stick is hung from a doorway.

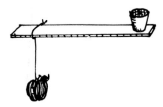

2. At the other end of stick, tack down one paper cup, placing tack through cup bottom and into flat side of stick as shown. Fill second cup ⅓ full of water, rice, etc.

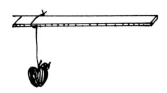

3. Tie one end of another string, about 2½′ long, around center of stick. Decide how far down stick should hang so apple may be comfortably reached. Tack loose end of string in center of doorway. Support hanging stick with one hand while setting second (filled) cup down inside the first.

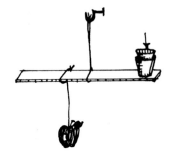

4. Still holding the stick, carefully slide apple string along it until it balances with the cups, as shown, step 3. Tie apple knot firmly in place.

5. Once stick is in balance, player may bob for the apple. Object is to bite the apple without spilling contents of cup. *Note:* When adding a new apple, hold stick so cup does not spill; adjust strings for balance.

APPLE PEEL FORTUNE

Materials: Apple, paring knife or vegetable peeler.

After you have bobbed for your apple, carefully peel it into strips as long as possible. Shut your eyes, throw peel over left shoulder and, in the shapes peel takes when it falls, you will read the initials of your true love.

Halloween superstitions having to do with nuts have been popular in England and Scotland since ancient times. In fact, Halloween is often called "Nut Crack Night" in these countries.

WALNUT BOAT RACE

Materials: Whole walnuts or halved walnut shells or tinfoil, table knife, Elmer's or Sobo glue, plasticene clay, toothpicks, paper, crayons or colored felt pens, scissors, large pan of water (in which to sail boats).

1. If using whole walnuts, break shells in half carefully by inserting point of table knife in flat end of nut as shown, and gently prying halves apart. Remove nutmeats.

(33)

2. If you do not have walnuts, boats may be made of tinfoil. Cut 7″ square of tinfoil. Fold in half (a), then in half again (b).

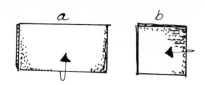

3. In center of each of the four sides, make a fold toward the inside. Press it over flat against the side, making a cup as shown, (a) (b) (c).

4. Fold points of cup over onto inside. Then fold down a narrow lip toward inside of rim, to secure. Press bottom of cup flat; press boat into shape with fingers.

5. To make sail, cut piece of paper 1½″ wide, 2″ long. Using crayons or felt pens, decorate with design or your name.

6. Stick sail onto toothpick as shown.

7. In center bottom of foil or nut boat, drop a small bit of glue, then press small ball of clay onto glue (a). When clay is firmly in place, stick to toothpick holding sail (b).

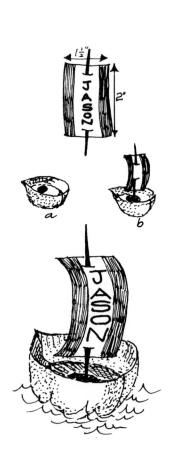

8. Set boat in water. To race, have each person at party, or in class, make a boat with his name on the sail. Hold boats at back edge of large tub of water. At starting signal, let boats go, players blowing evenly across sails to move boats. Whichever boat reaches other side of tub first wins.

(34)

Guy Fawkes Day

Because their dates are so close, the British Guy Fawkes Day, celebrated on November 5, has many customs in common with Halloween though in origin the holidays are unrelated. Guy Fawkes Day arose out of a religious conflict of the seventeenth century in England. When Roman Catholic priests were banished in 1604, several Catholic Englishmen organized a plot to blow up the Houses of Parliament in the name of religious freedom. They hid thirty-six barrels of gunpowder in the vaults of the buildings. On November 6, 1605, the plot was discovered and the conspirators tried and executed. Guy Fawkes is the individual most remembered because he had been chosen to set off the explosion. The gunpowder plot shocked the Protestant English, and at the time, only deepened their hatred of Catholicism. Guy Fawkes Day thereafter became a popular holiday on which people remembered the plot, confirmed their faith in the Anglican Church, lit bonfires, and burned straw dummies of Guy Fawkes and the Pope. Eventually, however, religious freedom returned to England.

Today, Guy Fawkes Day is mainly a holiday for children, who observe it by dressing up in funny costumes, having parades, lighting fireworks, and making straw dummies of Guy. Sometimes he is propped up on a cart on the sidewalk while the children who are his guardians beg "a penny for the Guy" from passersby; in some towns, Guy dummies are burned in bonfires.

Since the Gunpowder Plot of 1605, it has been a tradition on every Guy Fawkes Day for the Royal Yeomen of the Guard to prowl through the vaults beneath the Houses of Parliament in London in a mock search for the explosives. The Guardsmen are dressed in their traditional "beefeater" costumes (so called because they attend the King or Queen at state banquets) and carry lanterns to see clearly in the dark corridors. The following game, based upon this search, is especially fun for a large group.

(35)

YEOMEN OF THE GUARD HUNT

Before a Guy Fawkes Day party, the host should make *Guy Fawkes Firecracker Candies* (page 37) and hide them around the room. He should also hide a doll or straw dummy of Guy. A Yeoman of the Guard, or Beefeater, wears a colorful red costume with yellow and black striped trim, military medals on his chest, a black top hat, and a white neck ruffle. Each guest at the party may make, and wear, one part of this costume, the *Beefeater's Medal* described opposite. When medals are completed, each guest is given a flashlight (or one light to each pair of guests) and a small paper bag. Set a time limit, turn off the lights, and send the "guard" off to hunt for the "explosives" and for Guy. Prizes are given to whichever Yeoman, or pair, finds the most firecrackers. Whoever finds Guy is given a paper crown (see page 121), and presides over the rest of the party as the King or Queen.

GUY FAWKES FIRECRACKER CANDIES

Materials: Stick candies, red, yellow, and black crepe paper, scissors.

Cut narrow strips of red, yellow, and black crepe paper. Wind all three colors around the length of each stick of candy, twisting ends into tassles to hold.

BEEFEATER'S MEDAL

Materials: Colored construction paper, tinfoil, cardboard, compass (optional), scissors, safety pins, rubber cement, stapler, ruler, felt pens or crayons, pencil.

1. Cut two (or more) cardboard circles (see page 20, Method I or III), or trace around a half-dollar.

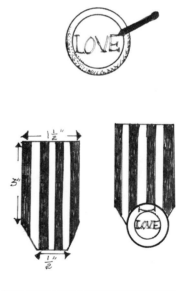

2. Cut tinfoil into roughly 2½″ squares (see page 20, Method I). Place one cardboard circle in center of foil square, fold foil over it to cover, and press foil flat on back side, making medal. With pencil, draw design or write inscription (what medal is for: PEACE, LOVE, BRAVERY, etc.) on front of medal.

3. To make "ribbon," cut strip of construction paper 3″ long, 1½″ wide. Taper bottom ½″ as shown. Decorate with paint or crayon stripes.

4. Staple or glue medal, front side out, onto tapered end of ribbon. Pin ribbon top onto shirt. You can make many medals and glue or staple them side by side onto a 1″-wide strip of paper as shown. Pin whole strip onto shirt.

(37)

Tết Trung-Thu

Tết Trung-thu, the Mid-Autumn Festival, is the biggest holiday of the year for the children of Vietnam. It is celebrated on the fifteenth day of the eighth month in the lunar calendar (September or October). Many of the festival's sweets, such as the traditional "moon cakes," are made in honor of the moon, which is full on this day. Moon cakes are made of sticky rice filled with different types of filling—for example, lotus seeds, peanuts, sugar, duck egg yolks, watermelon seeds, or raisins. The cakes are sold in decorative boxes and often given as gifts. It is generally believed that the festival had its origin in the eighth century A.D., during the reign of Emperor Minh-Hoang. Legend tells that on the fifteenth day of the eighth month, he took his Empress, Duong-Quy-Pho, to a beautiful lake, where he composed a poem and read it to her by the light of the full moon.

Lantern-making is the festival's primary activity. Children of all ages make lanterns of every description—boats, cranes, dragons, hares, unicorns, and carp, to name just a few. Lanterns are sold in the markets of every village. On the night of Tết Trung-thu, candles are lighted inside the lanterns, and the children form a procession, dancing through the streets to the music of drums and cymbals. It is said that this dance represents an imaginary trip to the moon. The illuminated lanterns glowing as they move through the night remind one of our own candlelit jack-o'-lanterns.

TẾT TRUNG-THU LANTERN

Materials: Flexible colored or white drawing, glazed, or origami paper, stiff white or yellow construction paper or bristol board (1-ply), stapler, scissors, pencil, rubber cement, cellophane tape, flashlight.

BIRD

1. Cut 9″ square of flexible white or colored paper (see page 20. Method I or II). *Note:* Dimensions may be easily enlarged, as long as bird is always made from a *square* and lantern from a *rectangle*.

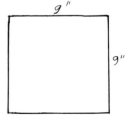

(38)

2. Fold square diagonally, as shown (a). Be sure when folding always to keep edges even. Fold triangle once again (b).

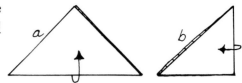

3. Now open the last fold, so you are back to step 2(a). With peak of triangle up, bend top layer down as shown, until its edge lines up with fold. This makes back part of wing.

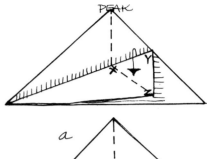

4. Holding point X, bend point Y down to the inside, under point X *until edges line up* (a). Press over fold, making wing. Tip is point Z (b).

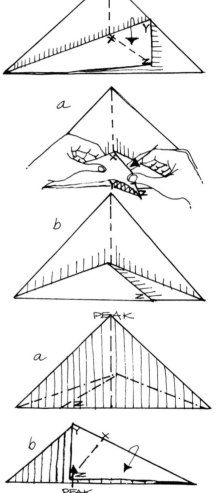

5. Turn paper over, so point Z is on underside to the *left*, and peak of triangle is up (a). Fold peak of triangle down as shown, until its edge lines up with fold, making back of second wing (b).

6. Holding point X, bend point Y down to the inside, under point X *until edges line up* (a). Press over fold, making wing; tip is point Z (b).

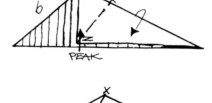

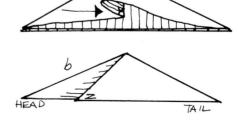

(39)

7. Holding tail closed, Z tips forward, push neck up, reversing its fold, as shown (a). Then grasp 2 side peaks formed at neck base and pinch together (b).

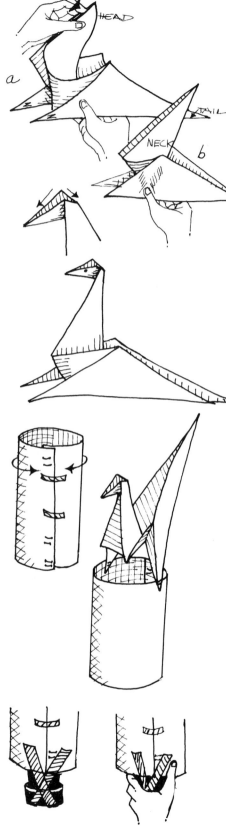

8. Still holding neck base, press head triangle tip down, forming head as shown. Press flat.

9. Completed bird, resting on wings.

LANTERN

1. Cut a rectangle of white or yellow stiff paper 8½″ by 11″. *Note:* Lantern must be white or yellow for light to come through. Pull short ends of rectangle around into a cylinder. Overlap edges about 1″ and staple ends together. Glue or tape side to hold closed.

2. Stand up lantern, seam in *back*, and staple, tape, or glue bird's wing tips onto inside of lantern top as shown.

3. To attach flashlight: Stand flashlight, bulb up, on table. Slide lantern down over it (with seam facing you) to within 2″ of light base. Tape seamed area to light base as shown. Grasp light base at this point to carry lantern.

4. To use lantern as centerpiece or light in room, simply stand flashlight, bulb up, on table. To hold steady, set it on a piece of plasticene or inside-out roll of masking tape. Slide lantern down over light.

Diwali

At the end of the autumn harvest season (usually late October or early November), Hindus all over India celebrate *Diwali* (dee-wah-lee), the "Festival of Lights." This is one of the gayest of all Indian festivals; both the northern and southern parts of the country have their own legends about the festival, but everywhere special honors are paid to the goddess of wealth and prosperity, Lakshmi. Special clay oil lamps, called *dipas* (dee-pas) or, in some places, elaborate brass oil lamps are prepared in every home. The flickering lamps are set out around the rooftops and along the windowsills of each house. In northern India, it is believed that each year at this time, Lakshmi returns from her summer in the country. With all the lights to guide her, she will surely find and bless every home as she passes through the countryside. In the city of Benares, women and girls silently float their lighted dipas across the Ganges River, hoping for good luck if the light still shines when it reaches the far shore.

On Diwali, stores and homes are scrubbed and decorated with flowers, special foods are prepared, new clothes worn, and fireworks displayed. Good luck designs, called *alpana* (al-pah-nah) are made on the ground or floor near the front door of the home. Special rice flour is used for the designs because rice once grew abundantly in India and so symbolizes abundance and welcome. In some areas, whole bits of rice are left in the flour for texture. The flour may be left white or mixed with dry color pigment. The designs may either be abstract or in such traditional folk motifs as the paisley. In north and northeastern India, the design is usually made with a liquid flour mixture dripped through the fingers into the pattern sketched on the ground or floor. In the south, dry flour is sprinkled onto the design. In some cities, competitions are held and prizes given for the most beautiful alpana.

ALPANA

Materials: Assorted colors of powdered poster paint, rice flour (optional), small bowls or tin cans (one for each color), wax paper, tinfoil, shallow stiff cardboard box or cigar box, scissors, dirt or sand.

1. Line box with tinfoil so dampness of dirt will not leak through. Fill lined box about half full with damp dirt (stones removed) or sand. Pack down flat and smooth.

2. Pour small amount of powdered paint and/or rice flour into bowl or can and mix. Prepare bowl of each color to be used.

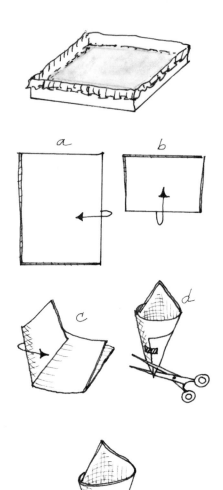

3. To make powder holders for each color: Cut a rectangle of wax paper 12″ by 16″. Bring short ends together folding paper in half (a). Keeping paper in same position, bring bottom edge up and fold in half again (b). With longest folded edge down, roll left side toward right, making cone. Keep tip *tightly* rolled and rounded (c). Tape end to hold cone together. With scissors, cut off about ⅛″ of tip, so opening is about ⅛″ across (d).

4. If desired, sketch design on scrap paper first. Or, with stick or pencil, sketch directly into packed dirt.

5. Plugging cone tip with your finger, pour some powder into cone (from mixture in bowl or can). Hold cone over the area where that color is wanted, unplug tip, and tap cone side gently as you trace it around design, dribbling out colored powder. Repeat until dirt is covered with colored powder design.

Rosh Hashanah and Yom Kippur

Several important holidays of the Jewish religion are celebrated in the autumn. As in biblical days, the New Year holidays, including *Rosh Hashanah* and *Yom Kippur*, are held at this time. They are followed closely by the autumn harvest festival of *Succot*.

The Jewish New Year is called *Rosh Hashanah,* or "Head of the Year." It is celebrated on the first two days of the Hebrew month of Tishri (September-October), and begins the "High Holy Days," the most sacred period of the Hebrew year, during which Jewish people devote themselves to prayer and self-judgment. The first day of Tishri is also special for another reason: Jewish legend tells that on this day the world was created, and in honor of this event, children in some religious schools sing "Happy Birthday, World" on this day. During the two days of Rosh Hashanah, many Jews do no work, but remain in the synagogue to pray. For this is the beginning of the Ten Days of Penitence during which God is believed to judge the lives of men and write his judgment down in the Book of Life. If you have lived a good life, your fate may be written on Rosh Hashanah, but if not, you are given the next ten days in which to concentrate on begging forgiveness from God, or whomever you may have wronged, for all sins. Promises are made to live a better life in the coming year. In a sense, this might be considered a religious form of the traditional "New Year's resolution."

Rosh Hashanah is also known as *Yom Teruah* (yohm-te-roo'-ah), the "Day of the Blowing of the Ram's Horn." Used since earliest times, this horn (in Hebrew, *shofar*) is known as the symbol of God's calling his people together— for self-improvement and self-judgment. According to the biblical story, the ram's horn is used because when Abraham was willing to sacrifice his son Isaac to prove the strength of his faith, God substituted a ram for the child. Today, the stirring sound of the shofar not only reminds Jews to repent for their sins, but also calls upon them to remember the ancient history and faith of their people.

In the home, Rosh Hashanah is celebrated with special foods. Honey cake, and apple slices and honey are eaten, with a special blessing for a "sweet year." The traditional *challah* (hah'-lah), or bread, is baked in a round shape, symbolizing the round, whole year. Sometimes it is shaped into a braid, or "ladder," or decorated with little birds and ladders, symbols to help prayers rise to

(43)

God. New fruits of the fall harvest are eaten, and *tzimmes* (tsim'-mes), a vegetable and meat dish, is baked. Besides sweet potatoes, meat, and prunes, tzimmes contains carrots, whose Yiddish name is *meyrin* (my'-rin), meaning "to increase," as the New Year should increase in goodness. Many Jewish people have adopted the modern custom of sending *Shanah Tovah* (good year) greeting cards to friends and relatives.

SHANAH TOVAH CARD

Materials: White or colored paper, scissors, ruler, pencil, tempera paint, brush, crayons or colored felt pens, ready-made envelope large enough to hold a 3″ by 5″ card.

1. Cut piece of paper 5″ by 9″.

2. With ruler, mark off 3″ sections along length of paper as shown.

3. Fold bottom third of paper up, and lightly pencil an X on edge as shown. This will later be erased.

4. Keeping *up* edge marked X, fold top third back and under it, as shown. Press along folds.

5. "Ladder-folded" card is now ready to decorate. Unfold, keeping X edge on *top*, and place flat on table. With paints or crayons, design your own decorations or copy those at right, *noting which parts of design go on which folded sections.* Erase X on top edge.

6. When design is dry, refold as in step 4. Place card in envelope and mail.

(44)

Yom Kippur, the "Day of Atonement," falls on the last of the Ten Days of Repentance begun on Rosh Hashanah. This tenth day of the Hebrew month *Tishri* is considered to be the holiest day of the Jewish year, the day on which God examines men's lives and their repentance of the previous ten days, and writes his final decision on their future in the Book of Life, which is then sealed until the next year.

In ancient times, the ritual of spiritual cleansing and atonement was closely associated with the harvest celebration of Succot. (See page 58.) In those days, men commonly believed that their characteristics could be transferred to animals. On this holiday, special ceremonies were held to give the evils of men to animals, called "scapegoats." Usually, two goats were chosen and after the rites, one was sacrificed and the other driven out of town. When the Temple of Jerusalem was destroyed in A.D. 70, animal sacrifice came to an end. Prayers said at that time were kept and continued, but today it is up to each individual to personally atone for his sins.

Yom Kippur is observed from sunset on the ninth to dark on the tenth day of Tishri. Adults and children over thirteen fast, businesses close, and no work is done by the Jewish community, who spend the day in the synagogue. During the service, the Book of Jonah is read from the Bible because it teaches a lesson in mercy and forgiveness. Jonah's story tells that God sent him as a messenger to tell the city of Nineveh that it would be destroyed because it was full of sin. To avoid this task, Jonah ran away to sea and boarded a ship. But God sent out a great storm to toss the ship, and the passengers and crew were terribly frightened. They cast lots to see who among them was to blame, and the lot fell upon Jonah. He then explained that the storm was his fault because he was running away from God. At his begging, the others threw him into the sea, and at once the storm stopped. God then sent a large fish to swallow Jonah. While inside the belly of the fish, Jonah remembered God and prayed to him, and as a result was cast out onto dry land. Again God asked him to go to Nineveh, and this time the humble Jonah delivered his message. The people of that city listened and repented, and because of this were not destroyed. But Jonah was angry because his prophecy was not fulfilled. God then explained to him the importance of forgiving people who repent their sins.

JONAH AND THE WHALE

Materials: Self-hardening clay, tempera paint and brush, shellac and brush, alcohol (shellac solvent), large (about 8″ by 10″) flat mirror or cardboard, table knife, newspapers, pencil.

Following the directions below, Jonah and the Whale may be made whatever size you consider appropriate for use as a table centerpiece or room decoration. Mirror or cardboard must be large enough to serve as base for the figures.

JONAH

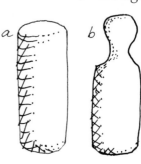

1. Read and follow directions on package of clay. This clay usually requires no special preparation; it is used as it comes from the package. Spread newspapers over work area. Model a clay cylinder the length of figure from head to bottom of torso as shown (a). Shape head and neck at one end (b).

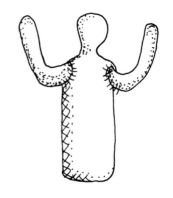

2. Make two clay rolls for arms. Attach arms firmly with slip (a creamy mixture of clay and water) at shoulders. Be sure arms are solid enough to remain outstretched as shown.

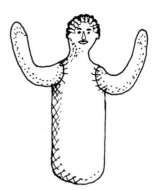

3. Hair and nose may be added to head with small bits of clay, drawn with pencil, or painted on later.

(46)

WHALE

1. Model thick rectangular solid as shown, length of whale from head to tail.

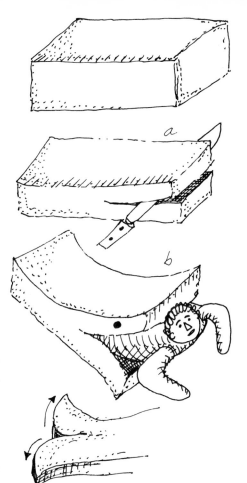

2. With knife, make mouth by cutting in from front of head as shown (a). Cut is about ⅔ length of head, long enough so when jaws are opened Jonah's body may be placed inside (b). Spread slip (see step 2 above) on insides of whale's jaws, set in Jonah's body as shown, and press in firmly, attaching to both top and bottom jaws.

3. To make tail, taper back end of rectangle, and with knife, cut width of tail in half as shown. Separate halves of tail.

4. Set Jonah and whale aside to dry. The clay dries without special firing in a kiln; it is completely dry when it turns a light reddish-brown (for terra-cotta clay) or light gray (gray clay) color, and "clicks" when tapped with a fingernail.

5. When clay is thoroughly dry, details may be painted on with tempera paint. *Note:* If more than one color is to be applied to a piece, allow the first to dry completely before adding the second. After tempera paint has thoroughly dried, pieces may be shellacked. Wash shellac brush in alcohol. Set completed figures on mirror "water" or, if using cardboard base, paint it with tempera to resemble water. Shellac painted base when dry.

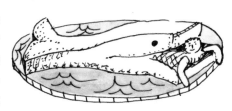

(47)

Thanksgiving

As long as men have grown their food, they have celebrated each harvest with a thanksgiving. The ancient Greeks and Romans honored their goddesses of grains and orchards with ceremonies including processions, music, song, sports, and games—all elements found in today's thanksgiving festivities. The ancient processions and harvest wagons, decorated with sheaves of grain, are related to our modern parade floats, and the pagan goddesses have their descendants in the "harvest queens" universally chosen to ride the floats or farm wagons at harvest time. In many countries, the harvest's last sheaf of wheat or corn is believed to be symbolic of the goddess of growing things and as such, is honored by being made into a goddess doll or *Kern Maiden* (see page 50), a bird feeder (see page 81), or a wreath for the harvest queen's crown.

Since the Middle Ages, the traditional harvest thanksgiving in Europe has been Martinmas, celebrated on November 11. This festival was named in honor of St. Martin of Tours who was born in the country now known as Hungary in the early fourth century. His pagan parents persuaded him to become a soldier, though Martin wished to convert to Christianity. While at Amiens, France, on military duty, a miracle is believed to have occurred that caused Martin's conversion to the Christian religion. One day he gave half his soldier's cloak to a freezing beggar, and that night Christ, wearing the half-cloak, appeared to bless him. After this vision, Martin converted, and later left the military to devote his life to religion. In the year A.D. 371, he was consecrated Bishop of Tours, France; later he founded a monastery outside Tours. On November 8, A.D. 397 or 400, he died in Candes, Touraine, and his elaborate funeral and burial were held at Tours on November 11, the day later honored as Martinmas. Throughout northern European and Scandinavian countries, Martinmas is still the occasion for a feast celebrating the harvest. Traditionally, roast goose is served, and in Sweden, the festival is called *Marten Gås* (mar-ten goohs), "Martin's Goose." With the goose, the first wine of the grape harvest, known naturally, as "St. Martin's Wine" is often served. It comes as no surprise to find that the ancient Romans celebrated a festival called the Bacchanalia on this same day in honor of Bacchus, god of wine.

On Martinmas in Germany and the Netherlands, children parade with lanterns made of scooped-out vegetables, similar to our pumpkin jack-o'-lanterns. In northeastern Switzerland, they are called *Räbenlichter* (raa'-bin-ligh-ter), meaning "turnip lights." Children make these lanterns of hollowed-out turnips, in which they carve designs or faces. A candle is placed in the center of each lantern, which is then hung on a stick and carried by a child in a parade, which wends its ways through the village streets to the gay folk tunes of a villager's harmonica.

RÄBENLICHTER (*Turnip Lights*)

Materials: Kitchen knife, spoon, yellow turnip, nail, wire, wire cutter, wooden stick with one notched end, newspapers, candle stub, matches.

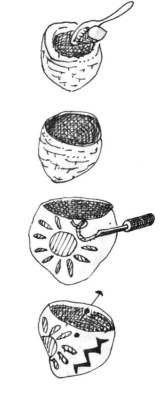

1. Spread newspaper on work area. With knife, cut circle in flat top of turnip. Remove this circle by cutting in small wedges.

2. With spoon, scoop out inside of turnip, leaving smooth bottom and walls.

3. Carve as you would a pumpkin, using table knife. Make face, or designs, all around turnip. *Note:* With a block printing tool, you can cut designs partially into the surface, but not puncturing it. These areas will be translucent when candle is lit inside.

4. With nail (or skewer), make two holes directly opposite each other in sides of turnip, about 1″ from top.

5. Push wire through holes and secure handle by twisting wire.

6. Melt wax on bottom of candle stub (with adult supervision) and drip a bit of wax into center bottom of turnip. While wax is still warm, set candle stub into position.

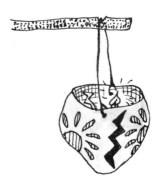

7. Hang wire on notch of stick and light candle. Or, prop lantern up on plate and use as centerpiece at Halloween or Thanksgiving party.

As previously mentioned, farmers of many countries preserve the last sheaf of harvested corn in the belief that it embodies the spirit of the corn goddess. On English farms, this sheaf is shaped into a doll or wreath and kept until the next harvest, to which it will hopefully pass on its fruitfulness. In Northumberland, this corn doll is known as a "kern baby," and she is crowned with a wreath of flowers. In other parts of England and Scotland, she is variously called a "corn dolly," a "kern maiden," and a "harvest queen."

KERN MAIDEN

Materials: Ear of corn with husks on, colored string or wool, glue or straight pins, oil-base felt pen.

1. Carefully peel husks halfway down corn. Fold husks down in half as shown. Remove silks.

2. Wind wool or string around the middle of ear, winding over husks in front and back and under all side husks. Tie thread in back. Raise side husks to make arms sticking out as shown. Tie several side husk tips together to form hands.

3. Glue or pin wool or string on top of ear for hair.

4. Draw face on front of ear with felt pen. Decorations may also be drawn on skirt husks.

Another popular English thanksgiving custom is the "Harvest Home." After the harvest has been gathered in, vegetables, fruits, flowers, and baked goods are brought to the churches and schools in the country where they are distributed to the needy. In the village of Westfield, Sussex, for example, boys and girls bring to school all varieties of foods and flowers. Each child writes a personal letter to someone poor or aged in the village. The letter is placed in a decorated basket along with a selection of the collected foods, and the baskets are then delivered to those less fortunate, teaching the children to share the real meaning of thanksgiving.

The American thanksgiving tradition, as you know, began with the Pilgrims, a group of men and women who left England and came to the New World in search of religious freedom. Their first year in their new home was a monumental struggle; for their survival, they owed much to the Indians, who were friendly and helpful, teaching them many new things such as how to plant corn. When the first harvest came in the fall of 1621, no men were more grateful than those Pilgrims who had survived. Their governor, William Bradford, decreed that a Thanksgiving celebration should be held, as it had been held back in England. But now it took on new meaning: it became a time to strengthen friendships with the Indian Chief, Massasoit, and his tribe in gratitude for their help; it was a time to thank God for their survival. Chief Massasoit and ninety of his braves were invited to that first feast, and they came bearing five deer as gifts. The Pilgrim men went hunting for wild birds and returned with many—including wild turkeys. The women prepared corn for the cornbread and cooked the feast over great open fires. For three days, the celebration continued. The Indians taught the settlers their games and together they raced, wrestled, sang, and danced.

INDIAN NUT GAME

Materials: Four flat-sided nuts (such as almonds with shells on) or four clean, dried peach or apricot pits. Tempera paint and brush, or colored felt pens, shallow bowl or dish.

1. Paint one side of each nut or pit red, the other blue (or any other color combination). Set to dry.

2. Give each color a number value. For example; red equals 2, blue, 1. (Instead of coloring sides, numbers may be painted on directly.)

3. When nuts are dry, place them in bowl. Each player takes a turn tossing nuts in bowl one time. The colored side or number which falls face-up gives the player's score. For example, if one red is up and three blues, score is 5. Highest score of each round wins. Or, whomever reaches score of 25 first.

STYROFOAM AND PINE CONE TURKEYS

Materials: Small (1″ or 2″ diameter) styrofoam ball, small pine cone, colored paper, scissors, colored pipe cleaners, map pins or small corsage pins, rubber cement, tempera paint, brush, carpet thread or thin wire, felt pen, exacto knife (optional).

STYROFOAM TURKEY

1. If desired, brush tempera paint over ball to color. Let dry. Make head and feathers (below) appropriate sizes to fit ball.

2. To make head: Bend pipe cleaner into a loop as shown. Press loop together to make face. Leave a small end hanging down for crop of turkey. Add eye on each side of head with felt pen.

3. To make feathers: Cut tail feathers in the same shape shown at right (a), making as large as necessary to look well on ball. Cut only two wing feathers (b).

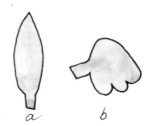

a   *b*

4. To mark tail feather lines, draw two or more semicircles around back of ball as shown.

5. Make slits along these lines with exacto knife (which is dangerous and should not be used without permission or adult supervision) or scissors point or pin point. Stick feathers (bottom down) in slits along each row. Press rows forward with finger to bend feathers upright.

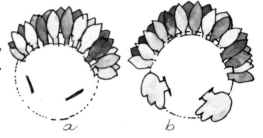

6. Make slit on each side of ball for wings (a), insert and fold wings forward along body (b).

a   *b*

7. Insert head in ball as shown, pushing pipe cleaner down into styrofoam.

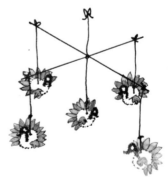

8. Press map or corsage pin into middle of turkey's back. Tie thread around head of pin, hang turkey up, or tie several turkeys onto a mobile (see page 124).

(53)

PINE CONE TURKEY

1. Make head, feathers, and wings as above. Dip ends of tail feathers in rubber cement and stick them between petals of pointed end of pine cone, as shown. When glue is dry, fold feathers forward slightly to make them stand up.

2. Glue wings and head in place as shown, wedging them in between petals of cone.

3. Stick pin into middle of back, tie on thread, and hang turkey up alone or on mobile.

The first *national* Thanksgiving Day in America was not proclaimed until 1789, when George Washington proclaimed it a day for giving thanks for successfully winning the War of Independence from England. It was a day to be grateful for the Constitution which the thirteen colonies had just written to bind themselves into a union and, in addition, it was a day to be grateful for the harvest. Though the dates varied, the colonists, and later the states, always observed a Thanksgiving feast following their harvest. But it was not until the Civil War, in 1863, that President Lincoln proclaimed a common date, the last Thursday in November, to be set aside for a National Thanksgiving Day. On this national holiday, Americans refrain from working, and gather with their families to enjoy the holiday feast including the traditional turkey, cranberry sauce, sweet potatoes, pumpkin, and mince pie.

(54)

Green Squash Festival

The Green Squash Festival, or *Wimákwari,* is celebrated in October by the natives of Huichol, Mexico. The principal decoration for this holiday is the wand, or *síkuli* with its woven design in the form of a "God's Eye," or *Ojo de dios* (oh'-ho day dee-os'). Although the Ojo de dios designs have become popular in Mexico for all occasions, they have special meaning for children on the day of the Green Squash Festival. The design symbolizes the eye through which the god, named *Kauyumáli,* sees the world. On this day, children carry the wands with the hope that the god will see them and grant them good health and long life.

OJO DE DIOS *(Eye of God)*

Materials: Two wooden sticks or dowels at least 6″ long (may be as long as 18″ for elaborate designs), several colors medium-thick wool, scissors.

1. Cross sticks in center, wrap end of wool over cross (a) and around side arms (b). Tighten ends A and B and tie together firmly (c).

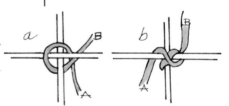

2. Holding ends A and B in position shown in (c) right, turn cross over, knot down. Again tie A and B together tightly, in double knot. Be sure sticks are firmly held in cross, not wobbly. Trim short end A, leaving B to make design.

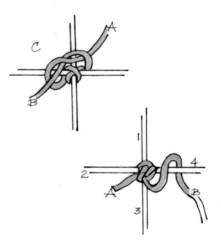

3. Holding cross sticks as shown, note numbers of each stick. Wind wool over stick 4.

(55)

4. Now pull wool *up* over *front* of stick 1, around it (a), and *down* over *front* of stick 2 and around it (b).

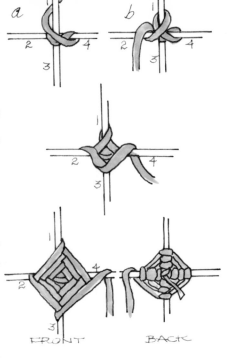

5. From stick 2, pull wool *down* over *front* of stick 3, around it, then *up* over *front* of stick 4 and around it.

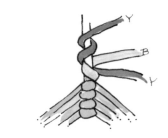

6. Repeat steps 4 and 5, winding wool over *fronts* of all sticks. After several turns, triangular "woven" pattern will be visible.

7. After working at least 1″ square of one color, another color wool may be added. To do this, place design face down, bring end of wool B to back of stick. Wind end of second color Y once around stick, then tie B and Y together. Be sure knot stays on back side of stick. Trim knot ends, leaving one end of Y for working design.

8. Design may be continued with second color, or other colors may be added. When design is as big as desired, turn face down, work end of wool over and under several strands on stick to hold. Trim end. Proceed to steps 12, 13, 14, and 15 to complete.

9. To weave a double pattern, first follow steps 1–7 above. Double method may begin any time after completing at least 1″ of single pattern. When you reach stick 4, at end of step 5, go over *front* of it, then around and *back up to back of stick 1 and around it*.

(56)

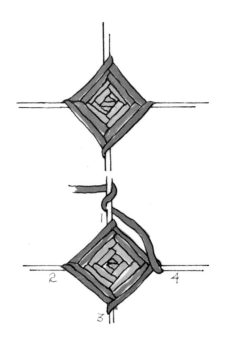

10. Wind down to *back* of 2, around it, down to *back* of 3, around it, and back up to *back* of 4. You have now completed first row of *back* layer.

11. Follow this by working another *front* layer. Pull wool around stick 4, up to *front* of stick 1, around it as shown. Continue, following steps 4 and 5. When you reach stick 4, go right into step 9 (last sentence), and step 10. *You must alternate front and back layers in this manner.*

12. After main portion of pattern is complete (step 8), shorter sticks may be placed on cross arms, and four smaller designs worked as shown.

13. To make fringe: Cut four pieces of wool, each 4″ long, for each stick, sixteen in all. Fold each piece in half.

14. Now cover stick ends by winding a piece of wool tightly up wood until 1″ from end (a). Place one folded piece of fringe (open ends *out*) against stick, wind once around folded end to hold; add second folded fringe further around stick and wind over its end as shown (b). Continue, adding four pieces of fringe around each stick.

15. To end, tightly wind wool *back over itself*, covering folded fringe ends. Turn design face down, lift one wound piece of wool from stick as shown and slip end through it (a). Pull end tight (b). Trim end.

(57)

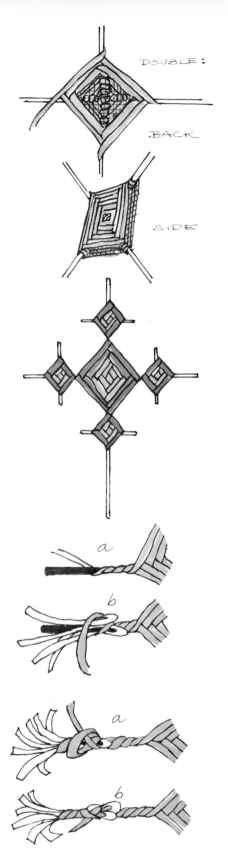

Succot

At the end of the autumn harvest, on the fifteenth and sixteenth days of the Hebrew month Tishri (September-October), Jewish people celebrate the "Feast of the Ingathering," or *Succot*. It is believed that this festival originated with the ancient Canaanite holiday after the grape harvest, during the autumn equinox, when rites were performed to encourage the rains. Boughs of fruit trees and evergreens were made into little booths in which the early Jewish farmers lived during the seven days of this celebration.

After the exodus from slavery in Egypt (see *Passover*, page 171), the wandering Jews lived in tents or booths, called "succot," pitched wherever they stopped for the night. Today, the holiday Succot is also called the "Festival of Booths," referring to both the ancient agricultural booths and those of the exodus.

A thanksgiving festival, Succot begins five days after Yom Kippur (see page 45) and lasts eight days. Jewish families traditionally make little booths, or *succot*, out of branches and leaves, decorating them with fresh fruits. Special blessings are said over the fruits in the succah. In Israel today, many families eat all their meals in the succah, and sometimes even sleep there. In the city of Jerusalem, contests are held and prizes given for the most beautiful succah.

FRUIT ANIMALS

Materials: Stiff colored foil or construction paper, straight pins, toothpicks, pencil, scissors, fresh fruit (lemons, oranges, apples, etc.).

Look at a piece of fruit and decide what animal it suggests to you, imaginary or real. Follow basic directions given, varying size and shape to suit your animal and fruit.

1. For a lemon animal (in our example): fold foil or paper 6″ long and 3¼″ wide in half, making folded piece 3″ by 3¼″; this will make head

and neck. (*Note:* Neck must be long enough to allow for ½″ bend at each end—dotted line in (a).) Draw animal's head and neck with pencil on one side of folded paper. Curve neck down as shown, and *keep nose on fold.* Draw eyes. Holding both sides firmly together, cut out head and neck (b). *Do not cut through nose fold.*

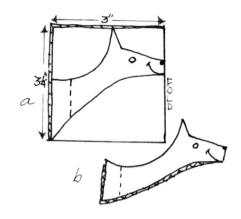

2. Cut single sheet of foil or paper 4″ long and 1½″ wide. Draw tail as shown, spreading the last 1½″ into a fan-shape which will fringe into curls (a). Cut out tail and cut into each fringe line. Curl up fringe (b).

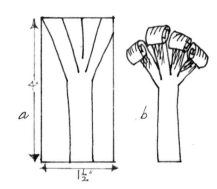

3. Open neck slightly and fasten head to fruit with straight pins or toothpicks. In example, folded neck base is pinned to either side of lemon stem.

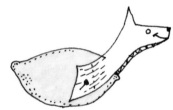

4. Pin on tail, stick toothpicks in fruit for legs. (If toothpicks are not strong enough to hold your fruit, use kitchen matchsticks with light-tips removed.)

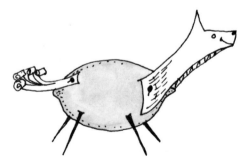

(59)

WINTER

To the earth's first men, the shortest day of the year, the winter solstice, was a time for celebration. For they knew it marked the time when days would begin to grow longer and warmer and spring would soon return. To encourage the sun's light to replace winter's darkness, most ceremonies included displays of firelight in the form of bonfires or torches. The importance of lighting has found its way into such modern Christian winter festivals as Christmas, and is perhaps not unrelated to the Jewish Festival of Lights, Chanukah, also celebrated at this time.

The ancient Romans held a winter festival on the seventeenth day of the last month of their year, December. Called Saturnalia, the holiday lasted seven days and was dedicated to Saturnus, the god of sowing, in honor of the completion of autumn planting. This was a holiday of abandon, gaiety, and freedom. Slaves wore their masters' clothes and were served by them. Courts and schools were closed, and the entire community celebrated. Presents, such as wax candles and terra-cotta dolls, were exchanged. In some provinces, lots were drawn to choose a mock "king" to play Saturnus during the festival. He was a clown, or "lord of misrule," whose duty was to amuse and entertain.

In northern Europe, the ancient Teutonic and Celtic tribes also held a winter solstice festival during their great feast month, December. The pagan Norsemen had a winter celebration lasting twelve days, called *jól*, or *hjul* (later "yule") meaning "wheel," the symbol of the changing seasons. Logs (yule logs) were burned and bonfires lit to brighten the darkest of days, to frighten away winter's demons, and to urge the sun to return. Decorations were made of holly, ivy, mistletoe, and evergreens, which bloomed throughout winter and so represented strength and life.

It is easy to see how many of our modern traditions originated with these ancient winter festivals. From the early tribes, particularly the Druids, Angles, and Saxons, come our decorations of evergreen, holly, ivy, and mistletoe, our yule logs, lights and candles, and our words "yule" and "yuletide." From the Romans come the customs of exchanging gifts and choosing a "lord of misrule" to preside over Twelfth Night festivities.

St. Nicholas Day

In the United States, everyone is familiar with red-suited, white-bearded Santa Claus who rides a sleigh pulled by reindeer and comes down the chimney on Christmas Eve bringing gifts to good children. This familiar character is related to the legendary European figure, St. Nicholas, who in countries such as Germany, Holland, Luxembourg, France, Switzerland, and Austria brings holiday gifts on his own day, December 6.

There are few facts and many legends about the life of St. Nicholas. We do know that he was born of a noble family in the city of Lycia in Asia Minor in the fourth century. His parents soon died, and he was raised an orphan. As a very young man, Nicholas decided to devote his life to religion. Because of his great piety, he was given an important church position while still young, and when he became the Bishop of the city of Myra, he was called "the Boy Bishop." Bishop Nicholas was especially kind and generous to children, as many legends show. Boys feel he is their patron saint because once he is said to have restored the lives of some boys salted in a barrel of brine by a wicked innkeeper. Girls love Nicholas because he is said to have helped three poor sisters. We are told that a poor man had three daughters whose dowries he could not afford. Without dowries, they could not be married, and the desperate man began to think of selling the girls into slavery. Bishop Nicholas heard the story, and one night secretly threw three bags of gold into the poor man's house, thus saving the daughters. This story has given rise to the popular belief that if girls pray to St. Nicholas, they will soon find good husbands. Nicholas performed miracles for ships at sea, and so became the patron saint of sailors, sea merchants, and the seaport city of Venice, Italy. The three bags of gold often appeared on ships and on sea merchants' coats of arms during the middle ages. When people began to borrow money from these rich merchants, the money-lender's symbol became three gold bags, or balls; and today, they have become the symbol of the pawnshop. Bishop Nicholas died on the sixth of December, either in A.D. 343, 345, or 350, and was immediately made a saint.

Tales of his miracles quickly spread from Asia Minor to the West, and by the year 450, churches in many countries had been built in his name. More than six hundred years after his death, Russians carried his legend back from Constantinople and he became the patron saint of Russia. From Russia, his stories spread to Lapland, home of the reindeer—and quite possibly the home of our

Santa Claus's reindeer. St. Nicholas became the patron saint of Greece, Sicily, and many European cities.

The modern St. Nicholas is portrayed slightly differently in each country, but generally he may be described as wearing a long white bishop's robe with a scarlet cape, a tall red mitre (bishop's hat), a white beard, and carrying a bishop's "pastoral staff." He rides a white horse or donkey, and has a helper, often dressed in black, whose job it is to punish, or threaten to punish, bad children with the birch switches he carries.

In France, for example, St. Nicholas (sahn nee'-koh-lah) places small toys in the shoes left out by children, while *Père Fouettard* (pair f'way-tar), the Bogeyman, scolds the bad, and often leaves them a bunch of birch twigs bound with a red ribbon as a reminder to behave. In Zurich, Switzerland, a parade is held on December 6 in honor of Sankt Niklaus, also called *Samichlaus* (sam'-igh-laos). Dressed as bishops, the boys in the parade wear long white robes and elaborately cutout paper headdresses in the shape of bishops' mitres. Transparent colored cellophane fixed inside the mitres give them the look of stained-glass windows.

ST. NICHOLAS HEADDRESS

Materials: White bristol board (4 pieces about 26″ by 18″), wax crayons, scissors, exacto knife (optional), ruler, colored cellophane, rubber cement, stapler, cellophane tape, old magazine, box of paper clips, pencil, tape measure.

MASK

1. To measure your head size for the mask, wrap the bristol board (26″ by 18″) *lengthwise* around your head, allowing bottom edge to rest upon your shoulders. Overlap ends until tube feels comfortably close to your head. (Eye, nose, and mouth openings will be cut later.) Mark, or have friend help you mark, where overlapping edges meet (arrow 1). Also mark where top of your head comes in tube (arrow 2).

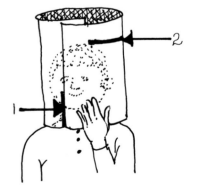

(62)

2. Spread out paper lengthwise on table, *marked side up,* with "top of head" mark at paper's top. Using a ruler, draw a line across length of paper at "top of head" mark (a). Then measure 3" *above* this line and draw a second line across paper as shown (b). Cut along this top line (b), and discard cut strip.

3. Along this top border, cut approximately 2" wide strips of fringe, as shown, cutting in *only* as far as "top of head" line.

4. Fold fringe down over line, as shown.

5. With marks on outside, pull the short ends of paper around as shown, making a tube. Fringe faces *out* from tube. Overlap edges of paper until they meet at marked point (see step 1). Hold edges together and staple at this point—once near the edge and a second time as far inside tube as stapler will reach. Fasten with cellophane tape along overlapped edges on inside and outside to hold edges where not stapled.

6. *With fringe end up,* place tube over your head. Rest bottom on shoulders and place seam in center of back. With fingers of one hand, press center front of tube against your eyes, nose, and mouth while with pencil in your other hand you *lightly (do not poke through paper)* mark these points on tube front. REMOVE TUBE FROM HEAD (a), and with scissors point, poke a small hole in each mark, then cut out the eye, nose, and mouth holes. Replace mask on head to test for correct shape and comfort; enlarge holes if necessary (b). With crayons, decorate features of face (c).

(63)

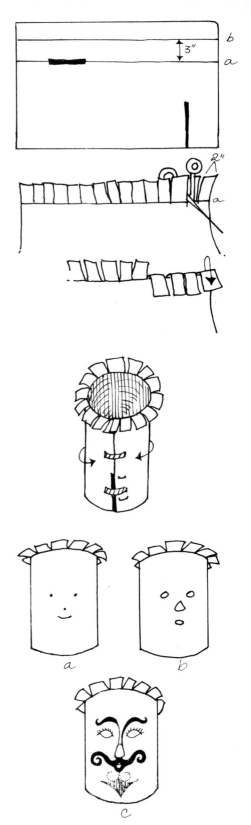

7. When face decoration is complete, set tube, *fringe down,* upon large piece of bristol board. Draw around edges of spread-out fringe, as shown (a). Cut out circle (b).

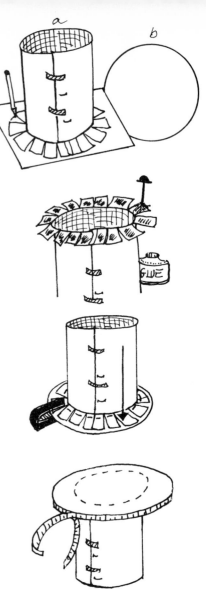

8. Turn tube *fringe end up* and spread rubber cement over *top* sides of each piece of fringe.

9. Turn tube *fringe side down* over paper circle, pressing glued fringe down as shown (arrow). Keeping tube in this position, staple each piece of fringe to circle, placing staples as close to tube as possible. Trim off any pieces of fringe that stick out over circle's edge.

10. Turn tube over, standing on open end. With tape measure, measure distance around edge of circular flat top as shown. (In example, distance is 42".) Divide this distance in half (21") to get measurement for the base of each half of headdress.

HEADDRESS

1. Headdress may be made as tall as you wish, depending only upon paper size. On scrap paper, first make a sketch of headdress, designing the curves as you wish. This will determine the shape and height of paper needed. (In example, hat will be 16" high *after* fastening base to brim.)

2. To make both halves of headdress, measure, mark, and cut out two pieces of bristol board—width determined in step 10 above (21") and height determined in step 1 above (16"). *Add 2" to height for brim attachment.* Total dimensions now are 21" by 18".

(64)

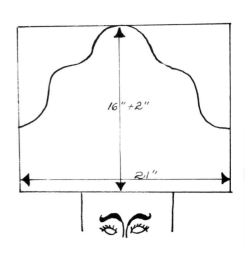

3. Place both halves of headdress side by side on table, *wrong side up.* To mark off brim, measure, mark, and draw a line across *length* of each paper 2″ in from edge as shown.

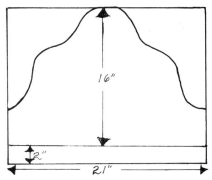

4. To shape headdress, work first with one half. Place paper lengthwise on table, and on both sides measure and mark points 6″ up from bottom. Above these 6″ marks, sketch, then cut out shape of top as you have designed or as shown. Place this cutout shape on top of second half of headdress and trace around outline. Cut second half to match first.

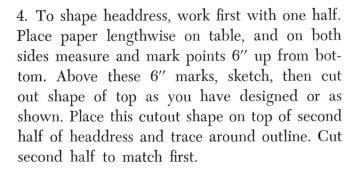

5. Headdress will now be decorated with "stained-glass" designs—that is, holes will be cut in the paper and covered with colored cellophane. Place one half of headdress *face down* on table. Sketch shapes to be cut out, or try different patterns out on scrap paper first. Keep shapes bold and simple, and remember to leave "ties" or links of paper between open shapes to connect them.

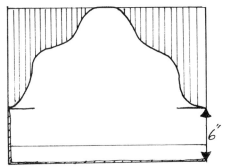

6. Draw design on wrong side of one half of headdress. Place old magazine underneath first shape to be cut. *Note: If using exacto knife, remember that blade is very sharp and should only be used with permission or adult supervision.*

7. Poke knife, or scissors point, through shape and into magazine below. Then proceed to cut shape out. Always keep magazine beneath paper if using the knife. If you mistakenly cut through a "tie" (see step 5), simply tape it back into place and cut away any visible tape.

(65)

8. After cutting out shapes on first half of headdress, set this over *wrong* side of second half and trace around cutout pattern. Following steps 6 and 7 above, cut out these shapes to match first half.

9. With *wrong sides of both halves* facing up, cover each hole with cellophane. To do this, hold a piece of cellophane approximately the correct size against each cutout hole and draw with crayon about ¼″ outside the shape's edge, so cellophane will be slightly larger than the hole it will cover. Cut cellophane shape out. Brush rubber cement over the edges of cutout hole and press on cellophane shape. Repeat for each hole in headdress. Rub off any rubber cement that gets on exposed cellophane.

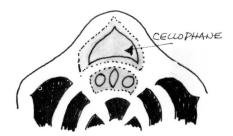

NOTE: The "stained-glass" design may be considered complete at this point, or if desired to make the colors appear brighter, a piece of white paper may be glued over entire wrong sides of headdress. To do this, trace around outside edge of each half on white paper, cut out, and glue paper over back of each half.

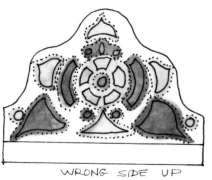

WRONG SIDE UP

10. Place both halves of headdress *face up* on table. Fold the 2″-wide brim of each half up along marked line, pressing it onto front as shown.

11. Now fold brim in half, bending its top edge down toward you until it lines up with bottom fold, as shown. Press along fold.

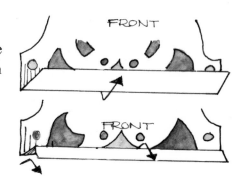

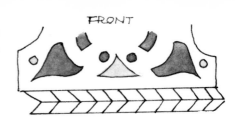
FRONT

12. Unfold brim and cut approximately 2″-wide strips of fringe as shown, cutting in *only* as far as brim line.

13. To attach headdress to mask, stand mask, open end down, on table. With face in front, center one half of headdress on flat top directly over face, and paper clip the folded fringes *over* edges of flat top as shown.

14. Repeat step 13 with back half of headdress, which is centered over tube seam. Overlap sides of two halves where they meet, and staple them in place at the top. Tape edges together on bottom of inside to hold firmly.

15. One by one, remove each paper clip and staple the folded fringe onto flat top brim as shown. Completed headdress may be worn with long white robe.

In Sweden, after the Christmas Eve feast, the family awaits the arrival of the *Jultomten* (yul-tom′-tehn) or Christmas elf, who rides a sleigh drawn by the *julbockar* (yul-bok-kar), or Christmas goats. With his white beard, red stocking cap, and red suit, the Jultomten resembles our modern Santa Claus. He carries a sack full of goodies, and hopes to find a bowl of porridge set out for him in the barn by considerate children.

In Stockholm, the capital of Sweden, there is a very busy shop called *Tomteloftet*, meaning "Santa's Workshop." Here post offices around the world forward letters addressed to "Santa Claus, North Pole." All the letters are answered, and often small gifts made by Swedish primary school children are

(67)

enclosed, along with the child's name and address. If you write to Santa (his correct address is "Tomteloftet, Skansen, Stockholm, Sweden"), you will be answered, and may even discover a new Swedish friend.

When Dutch seamen brought the legend of St. Nicholas back from Myra to Holland centuries ago, they named him "Sint Nicolaas" or "Sinter Klaas." On the eve of Sint Nicolaas' Day, he makes his rounds riding a horse called *Sleipnir*. He is accompanied by a helper, called *Zwarte Piet*, or "Black Pete," who punishes the bad children. When the first Dutch settlers came to Niew Amsterdam (now New York), they brought with them all the customs related to their Bishop Sinter Klaas. In the new land, he quickly grew to look more like a Dutchman, with his knickers, boots, and pipe, than the somber bishop of Europe. From Sinter Klaas our modern Santa Claus evolved, his sled pulled by reindeer instead of the Dutch horse.

Our tradition of Santa Claus coming down the chimney began with the ancient Norsemen's winter solstice festival in honor of the goddess of the home, Herthe. Before the holiday feast, a fire of fir boughs was laid on an altar of flat stones. It was believed that Herthe would appear in the smoke to bring good fortune to the home. The Norse altar stones became our modern "hearthstones," and the chimney the place for Santa, instead of Herthe, to appear.

Santa Claus's American image was not entirely fixed until Dr. Clement C. Moore wrote his famous poem, "A Visit from St. Nicholas," on December 22, 1822, and drew the sparkling portrait of our modern Santa Claus.

ST. NICHOLAS   BLACK PETE   JULTOMTEN   SANTA CLAUS

(68)

St. Lucia Day

The Christmas season in Sweden, and in Swedish communities throughout the world, begins on December 13 with *Luciadagen* (loo-see'-ah-dah-gen) or "Lucia Day." This is the Festival of Light in honor of St. Lucia who, according to various legends, was a young girl who lived in Sicily about A.D. 300. Because she insisted on remaining a loyal Christian, she had her eyes put out and was executed by the Romans, under Emperor Diocletian. For her martyrdom on December 13, Lucia was made a saint, the patroness of the blind. She is buried in the Church of Santa Lucia in Venice, Italy.

According to the early calendar, Lucia's Day fell on the shortest day of the year, the winter solstice. In Scandinavia, this was the joyful day after which winter began to turn into spring; when the Vikings were Christianized, they adopted the Italian saint as the day's patroness because her name, *Lucia*, meant "light." Lucia inherited many of the pagan light and fire customs of this day, and thus became the "Light Saint." Belief in her power to break winter's spell gave rise to a popular Swedish folk custom. On the eve of her day, children write the word *Lussi* (Lucia) on doors and fences, along with a drawing of a girl. Their hope is that Lussi will work her spell and drive away winter, just as in ancient times, signs were placed outdoors to announce to winter's demons that their strength was broken and the sun would soon return.

Today, Luciadagen is celebrated in every Swedish home. At dawn, the eldest daughter, who represents Lucia, dresses in a white gown with a crimson sash. She wears a crown of greens topped by real candles. Singing the traditional Italian melody, "Santa Lucia," she is followed by her younger sisters, also in white gowns, but without crowns. Lucia carries a tray of coffee and festive *Lucia buns* to the rest of the family. The buns, especially baked with saffron flavoring, have many traditional shapes. The most common are the *Lussekatter* or "Lucia cats." A good-luck symbol since ancient times, the cat was a sign to keep the devil out of the house, for he was thought to appear in the form of a cat.

In some towns, "Lucia" and her costumed attendants go from house to house singing, and serving coffee and Lucia buns. Recently, the custom of holding Lucia beauty contests has grown, and in cities, offices, and clubs, the prettiest girl is chosen to be "Lucia."

(69)

LUCIA BUNS

Lucia buns are made of yeast dough flavored with saffron, which gives a yellow color and special flavor. A simple sugar cookie dough stiff enough to be shaped with the hands may also be used. Follow *Swedish Vanilla Cookie* recipe, page 82, adding (at the same time as vanilla extract) several drops of yellow food coloring. Use raisins for decoration, shaping the dough into the following special *Lucia Day* shapes.

LILJA *(leel'-ya)*—Lily

1. Shape one roll 7″ long.

2. Bend it in half, curling up ends as shown, into lily shape. Place raisin in center of each curl.

3. With floured or sugared spatula, transfer to greased cookie sheet.

POJKAR *(poy'-kara)*—Boys

1. Shape one roll 8″ long.

2. (a) Bend roll in half, placing right leg over left, as shown.

   (b) Gently twist leg now on right, over left.

   (c) Repeat step (b).

3. With floured spatula, transfer to greased cookie sheet.

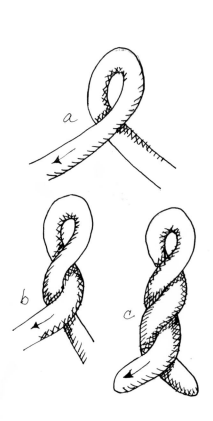

(70)

LUSSEKATTER *(looh'-sah-kah'-tor)*—Lucia Cats

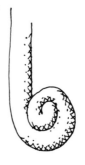

1. Shape one roll 10″ long.

2. Curl one end of roll around itself as shown, keeping curl on bottom.

3. Bend roll down, then curl up other end against first, as shown.

4. Place raisin in center of each curl. With floured spatula, transfer to greased cookie sheet.

KRONA *(kroo'-nah)*—Crown

1. Shape five rolls 3″ long.

2. Curve one roll gently around to form base.

3. Curl four remaining rolls as shown.

4. Set curls on base, pinching ends gently to set. *Note:* Two curls on left face two on right. Set raisin in center of each curl. With floured spatula, transfer to greased cookie sheet.

Christmas

The winter festival of the pagans received a new name (in Old English, *Christes Mæsse* or "Christ's Mass") and a new meaning with the coming of Christianity. However, the date of the celebration of Christ's birth varied for many years. There is no record of the exact birth date of Christ. Church history before the fifth century could not agree upon a date to celebrate, and alternated between March 25, March 28, November 17, December 25, and January 6. Not until A.D. 354 was the first certain mention made of December 25 as Christ's birth date, and as this was the date of the Roman Mithraic feast in honor of the sun, opponents of the date claimed Christ was being associated with sun worship. In any case, it was not until A.D. 440 that the church fathers finally decided to set the most important Christian festival, Christ's birth, at the same time as the important pagan celebration, the winter solstice. Thus, as Christianity spread, it was easier to make substitutions: pagan temples were converted into Christian churches, pagan customs took on Christian meanings. The bonfires, candles, and yule logs lent their legends to Christ, "the light of the world," and the holiday gradually became Christmas as we know it today, a combination of religion and folk custom.

The transition from pagan to Christian can be clearly seen in the folklore of the Christmas symbols. Holly was worshipped by the ancient Druids, who saw that it remained green and even bore fruit (red berries) in winter, a sign that life would go on, and the sun return. Holly thus became the symbol of immortality. Holly was also believed to be hateful to witches, and even today in many countries, holly branches are hung over doors, windows, and fireplaces to keep witches away. In some parts of England, it is said that bees hum a carol on Christmas Day in honor of the Christ Child. Holly is placed on the hives to wish the bees a Merry Christmas.

HOLLY PLACE CARD

Materials: Red and green construction paper, scissors, pinking shears (optional), rubber cement, pen.

1. Trace pattern A (page 81), transfer (see page 18) three times onto green paper. Trace pattern B (page 81) three times onto red paper. Trace and transfer pattern C (page 81) once onto either color paper. Cut out all pieces, using regular or pinking shears.

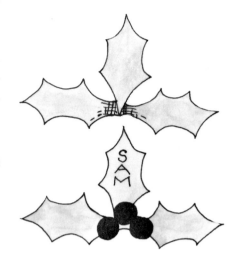

2. Glue ends of three green leaves together as shown.

3. Glue three red circles onto leaves.

4. With pen, write guest's name on center leaf.

5. Fold up strip C on dotted lines. Fold over short end, glue as shown. Then brush glue over front of this same side and press on center leaf of holly. Stand holly card at party table to show guests where to sit.

NOTE: If you are fortunate enough to have real holly, simply glue three leaf sprays onto stand made of strip C (step 5). Write name on leaf with oil-base felt pen.

Mistletoe also was sacred to the Druids, who called it *misteltan*, meaning "different twig" since, semiparasitic, it lived off of the trees it grew upon. They believed mistletoe had the power to protect one from evil, give great strength, and even encourage fertility. In Scandinavian countries, where mistletoe stands for friendship and peace, it is believed that if enemies meet beneath the mistletoe, they will put down their arms and be friends until the next day. In England, when mistletoe hangs overhead, a boy may kiss a girl beneath it. He then removes a berry and gives it to her, but when all the berries are gone, the branch loses its power and no more kisses can be given. *Note: Do not eat mistletoe berries; they are poisonous.* In Sicily, bouquets of mistletoe are sent to friends at Christmas, and twigs are hung over doorways for good luck. In the United States, of course, mistletoe is hung in doorways and whoever passes beneath it is liable to be kissed.

MISTLETOE HOLDER

Materials: Scissors, stapler, mistletoe, miniature decorative bells, thumbtack, one flexible cardboard strip *or* stiff straw ribbon (1″ wide, 30″ long), and ribbons: 1 red ribbon ¾″ wide, 24″ long; 4 red ribbons ¾″ wide, 1 yard (36″) long; 1 gold ribbon ¾″ wide, 4 yards long.

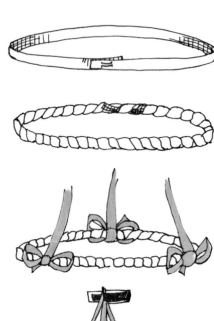

1. Bend straw or cardboard strip around into circle, overlap ends about 1″ and staple as shown.

2. If you have used cardboard, cover it with gold ribbon. Begin by taping one end of ribbon to inside of hoop; then wrap it neatly, overlapping edges slightly, until entire hoop is covered. Tuck end under strip of ribbon on inside, and glue in place.

3. At three evenly spaced points on hoop, tie on one end of a yard-long red ribbon. Make bow at hoop end (bow uses about 16″ of ribbon).

4. Gather tops of these three ribbons, adjust ends until hoop hangs evenly. Slip one end of fourth yard-long ribbon among these ends, so fourth ribbon hangs down in *center* of hoop. Holding all ends firmly, staple together.

5. Tie remaining red ribbon over stapled ends and into bow, from which hoop will hang.

6. Tie end of central ribbon onto mistletoe. It should hang down slightly below hoop.

7. With carpet thread, tie small bells onto hoop *between* bows. Hang mistletoe hoop from ceiling or doorway with thumbtack.

(74)

Just as the early Norse tribes burned their "yule" logs to frighten away winter's demons, the Druids of the British Isles prayed that the oak or fruitwood log burned in their midwinter festival would flame, like the sun, forever. A piece of this burned log was saved to start the next year's fire. The log, or its ash, in this case was symbolic of the fire-sun and its protective powers, and served as a symbol of good luck and strength, protecting one from evil spirits. Even today in many countries, a bit of the yule log or ash is still preserved until the following year. In Yugoslavia, ashes of the yule log are buried under the roots of the fruit trees to make them bear more fruit. In some parts of the British Isles, the yule log's ashes are kept as a good-luck token until the following winter. The English yule log is said to be related not only to the Druids, but also to the medieval custom of having the Christmas banquet last as long as a "wet wheel," or green log, burned in the open hearth of the great dining hall. Today, yule logs are still burned on Christmas Eve, and often are kept burning, or are rekindled, throughout the holiday season.

We know that evergreen boughs were used in pagan ceremonies long before the coming of Christianity, but it is possible that the use of a symbolic *tree* may have an even earlier source. The ancient Egyptians observed a midwinter festival in honor of the god Horus, son of Isis, the goddess of motherhood and fertility. The symbol for the celebration was a palm tree with twelve shoots; their palm put forth a shoot each month, and a tree with twelve shoots therefore stood for the complete year. Legends abound explaining the modern origin of the "Christmas" tree. One tells that Martin Luther, leader of the Protestant Reformation in sixteenth-century Germany, was walking in the woods on Christmas Eve. With the snow underfoot and the stars twinkling overhead, the woods were hushed and wondrous. He came upon a small fir tree covered with snow, cut it down, and brought it home for his children to share its beauty. Candles were placed upon the branches to represent the stars. Another explanation tells that Christmas Eve was celebrated by the Eastern Orthodox Churches as the Feast Day of Adam and Eve. This observance spread to the West, where in Germany in the sixteenth century, there developed the custom of decorating a "Paradise Tree," a fir tree covered with apples, in honor of Adam and Eve. It is generally accepted that our modern Christmas tree had its origin in northern Europe, probably Germany, and from there the tradition spread throughout the Christian world. The German Prince Albert brought the custom to England when he married Queen Victoria, and German immigrants first brought the tree to the United States.

Wherever there are Christmas trees there are decorations; they vary from

(75)

one country to the next, but always, the most interesting and imaginative are those made by hand. In Austria, although more elaborate ornaments are also used, it is traditional to decorate the tree with oranges, apples, and nuts wrapped in silver or gold foil, a custom perhaps related to the "Paradise Tree."

AUSTRIAN NUT DECORATIONS

Materials: Assorted whole nuts (pecans, walnuts, almonds, Brazil nuts, etc.) gold or silver tinfoil, thin wire or narrow red string. *Note:* Apples and oranges are too heavy to hang on most fir trees.

1. Cut foil into squares large enough to wrap completely around nut. Place nut in center of foil and wrap, twisting ends of foil together as shown.

2. Tie wire or string around foil; then tie ends of string together to make a loop. Hang covered nuts on tree.

The Christmas decorations of tropical regions, such as Hawaii, are often made of palm fronds, or leaves. The following decoration can be made of either paper or palm.

HAWAIIAN KINIPOPO

Materials: Two coconut palm fronds (with *niau*, or midrib, removed) about 12″ long *or* two strips colored paper, each 1½″ wide, 14″ long, carpet thread, scissors.

1. If using paper, fold strips lengthwise down center, making each side of strip ¾″ wide.

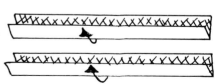

2. Cut down fold of each strip to within ½″ of bottom, which *must* remain joined. Cut angle at base as shown.

3. With either palm or paper, place the two V-shaped pieces over each other as shown, so pointed bases are down and leg 2 comes between legs 3 and 4.

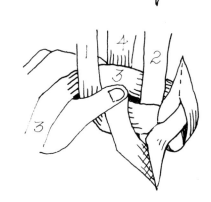

4. Take leg 1, which is on right edge, and keeping it *flat*, place it *behind* leg 3, then in *front* of leg 2, then *behind* leg 4. Hold the work firmly as you weave, and keep woven strips as close together as possible.

5. You will see bases of strips begin to curl up. Leg 3, which is now on right outside edge, is treated as if it were old leg 1 and step 4 above is repeated: *leg 3 is placed behind, in front, then behind the next three legs.*

6. Continue to repeat step 4 above, always treating the leg on right edge as if it were leg 1, weaving it through the legs beside it. Remember to keep legs flat, and let work curl up on itself. After three legs are woven, work will look like this.

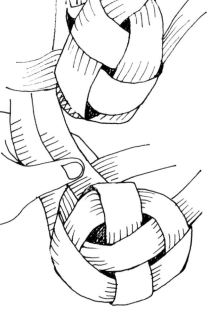

7. Continue weaving until ball is formed, with base points well hidden inside.

(77)

8. When ball is completely formed, hold ends firmly in directions they are now facing and tuck them into slots following the direction of the weave—over, under—until ends are out of sight; or, cut them off after tucking through at least one slot to hold.

9. Tie thread through ball and hang up on tree. Or, if palm was used, spray with colored enamel if desired. Several balls may be hung on a mobile.

Candles, a symbol of light, have been popular since ancient men lit them hoping to magically dispel the darkness of winter. For the early Christian, candles symbolized Christ's "light" which replaced the "darkness" of paganism. It has long been a custom for special candles to be lit during the Christmas holidays. In medieval Europe, giant candles were lit at Christmas and allowed to burn continuously until Twelfth Night. Pre-Christmas candles are also important, and the tradition of lighting Advent candles during the four weeks before Christmas is popular in many countries. In Austria, Catholics observe the coming, or "advent," of Christ's birth by attending church every morning at six o'clock during the four weeks. This is a solemn period during which one prepares his conscience for the beginning of Christmas. On each of the four Sundays, a special candle is lit on the *advent kranz,* or advent wreath.

ADVENT WREATH

Materials: Red birthday candles or "flower tapers," evergreen branches, flexible wire, 4 candlesticks (all same size) or 4 large empty carpet thread spools (painted red with tempera paint).

1. Wind wire several times around, making a circle the size of finished wreath.

(78)

2. Set 4 candlesticks, or spools, evenly spaced around wreath between loops of wire. Twist short extra pieces of wire first around candlestick base then around wire loop, to hold candlestick in position.

3. To attach greens, twist a piece of wire over each evergreen stem and then twist it onto loop. Overlap short twigs of greens, making a full, bushy wreath covering the candlestick or spool bases.

4. Carefully bend under any exposed wire ends. *Note:* To make birthday candles fit spools, wind narrow strip of tape around candle base; "flower tapers" may need their bases shaved slightly to fit spools. Light one candle the first Sunday, one more each Sunday, for four weeks until Christmas, when, on the final Sunday, all four are lit. Replace candles if they burn out.

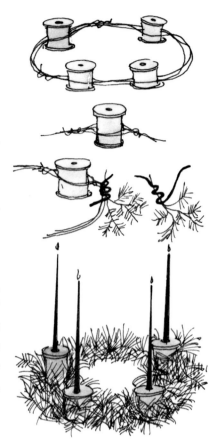

The Christmas tree did not come to Scandinavian countries until the early nineteenth century, but today there are trees in every Christian home and even trees tied to the masts of Danish ships at sea. Christmas Eve is the gayest holiday night in Denmark. After Church, the family shares a holiday feast including roast goose and a traditional rice pudding containing a hidden almond. Whoever finds the almond in his portion receives as a prize a *marzipangris* (mar-zi-pan'-grees), or marzipan pig (see page 98). A bowl of porridge is placed in the stable to please the goblin *nisse* in the hope that he will remain another year to guard the barn. A sheaf of grain is placed on a pole outside for the birds' Christmas feast. After dinner, the children are shown the Christmas tree for the first time. The decorations are often homemade in traditional patterns.

JULEHJERTER *(yul-a-yehr-tah)* Danish Christmas Hearts

Materials: Red and white construction paper, rubber cement, darning needle, carpet thread, scissors, pencil, ruler.

 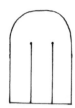

1. Trace pattern D, page 81, and transfer (see page 18) once to red paper, once to white. Cut out both pieces, which should be exactly same size.

2. Cut along transferred strip lines, making three strips on each piece. *Do not cut beyond marked lines.*

3. Place white *piece* over red, *lining up edges as shown* (a). Begin weaving with top white strip, marked X, bending it *over, under* then *over* red strips (b). Work second white strip *under, over, under* red (c). Third white strip follows first. Line edges up. Glue ends with rubber cement if necessary to hold in place. *Note:* Woven design may be made smaller by cutting the three strips each in half, making six strips on each side of heart. Weave as above.

4. Thread darning needle with carpet thread, take stitch in top of woven heart, pull thread up and tie into loop. Hang heart on tree.

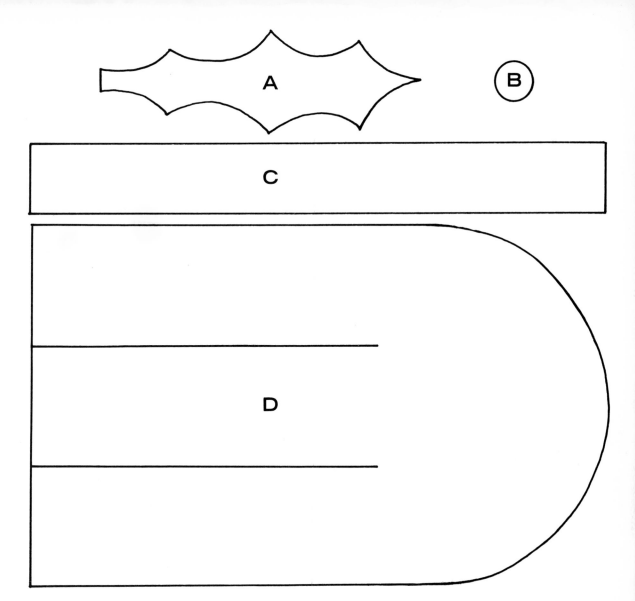

In Sweden, as in Denmark and Norway, there are traditions of sharing the Christmas feast with the birds. The Swedish save a sheaf of grain, usually oats, from the fall threshing to tie onto a pole outside for the birds. In Norway, melted suet and birdseed are formed into blocks, tied onto sticks, and placed outside in the snow.

SCANDINAVIAN BIRDFEED

Ingredients: 1 lb. suet
1½ cups birdseed

Equipment: Spoon, frying pan, empty 1-quart milk carton (top removed), red cotton string, paper towels.

1. Crumble or cut suet into small pieces in frying pan. Cover pan and set on *low* heat to melt suet. When checking to see if suet is melted, do not stand too close to pan, for hot suet "spits."

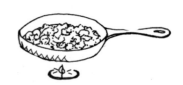

2. When all fat is melted, and only a few small crisps of suet remain, turn off heat. Let pan sit for about 25 minutes until cool.

3. You now have about 1 cup melted suet. Add to this 1½ cups birdseed. Mix gently. Let mixture sit an hour, until cold but not solid.

4. Spoon cold mixture into milk carton. Wipe outside of carton with paper towel and place overnight in refrigerator.

5. Next day, when suet has hardened, peel off carton. Place solid suet-seed cube on paper towel.

6. Tie with red string as you would a package.

7. Tie ends of string around branch of tree for birds.

Christmas cookies and cakes are an important part of holiday festivities in all countries. In Sweden, there is an old custom that a Christmas cake should be saved until spring, when it is thrown in front of the plow to insure an abundant harvest. Swedish baked goods, and especially cookies, are formed into traditional shapes for Christmas.

BRYSSELKÄX *(bree-sel-kehx)* Swedish Vanilla Cookies

Ingredients: 1 cup (2 sticks) sweet butter   2 tablespoons vanilla extract
(leave out of refrigerator until soft)
½ cup sugar   confectioners' sugar
2½ cups flour sifted   raisins
(*Note:* 1 tablespoon almond extract may be substituted for vanilla)
Makes about 30 cookies

Equipment: Measuring cup and spoons, large mixing bowl, sifters, spoon or electric beater, spatula, kitchen knife, greased cookie sheets, apron, ruler or tape measure.

1. Preheat oven to 350°. Grease cookie sheets with shortening and set aside.

2. Wash hands thoroughly before mixing and handling dough. In mixing bowl, using spoon or beater, blend sugar and butter.

3. Add vanilla extract and mix.

4. Add sifted flour, ½ cup at a time, mixing well. After adding last ½ cup, mix dough—which will be very stiff—with your hands. When dough is thoroughly blended, shape into ball and remove from bowl.

5. Set dough on lightly floured (or confectioners' sugared) board or counter. Dip hands in flour or confectioners' sugar before shaping dough as shown below.

NOTE: (a) If dough breaks or cracks while shaping, pinch or pat it back together, or roll lumps of dough in hands to warm butter slightly, making dough more pliable.

(b) "Rolls" of dough referred to in all shaping directions are rolled like clay "snakes," to about ⅜" thickness, unless otherwise specified.

6. When placing cookies on cookie sheet, space them out so there is room for them to spread in baking. Bake about 5 minutes, until golden. When cool, remove to serving plate.

KORS *(korsh)*—Cross

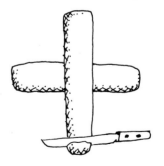

1. Shape two 3"-long rolls of dough.

2. Place one roll over the other in a cross. Press gently in place. Trim ends straight with knife.

3. Shape two "pencil-lead" thin rolls, each 3″ long. Press one roll over each arm of cross, as shown.

4. Dip spatula in flour or confectioners' sugar, slip under cross, and transfer it to greased cookie sheet.

STJÄRNA *(sheher-nah)*—Star

1. Shape one 14″ long roll. Bend roll in half.

2. 2″ down from peak, bend right leg up as shown, crossing it over left leg. Pinch angles slightly to neaten.

3. Repeat step 2 with left leg, crossing it over right.

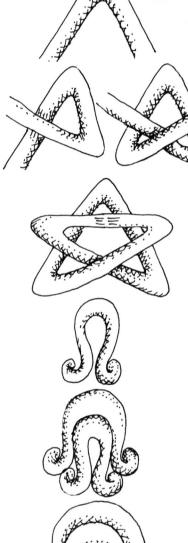

4. Bend and bring in the two unattached legs, pinching them together below peak of star, as shown. With floured spatula, transfer to greased cookie sheet.

PRÄSTENS HÅR *(pres'-tons hoor)*—Priest's Hair

1. *Note:* These may be shaped directly upon cookie sheet if desired. Shape three 7″-long rolls.

2. Bend first roll in half as shown, curling ends over.

3. Place second roll over top of first and shape as shown.

4. Add third roll above second. Be sure all ends are neatly curled. Place raisin in center of each curl. With floured spatula, transfer to greased cookie sheet.

(84)

KYRKODÖRR *(sheer-kah-dahr)*—Church Door

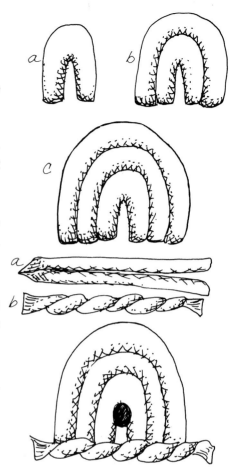

1. Shape three rolls, one 3″ long, one 4″ long, and one 5″ long.

2. Curve shortest roll in half as shown (a). Curve 4″ roll over it (b), and 5″ roll over that (c). Trim ends even with knife.

3. Shape two 4″-long rolls; place them side by side, pinch ends together (a) and twist rolls together (b).

4. Center twist at base of curved rolls; press them together lightly to join. If desired, place raisin in center of smallest curve.

5. With floured spatula, transfer to greased cookie sheet.

Christmas is a colorful religious festival in Mexico. The holiday begins on December 16 with the traditional "posada" (poh-sah′-dah), meaning literally "inn" or "shelter"; posadas are processions, held in village streets, churches, and homes, which commemorate the eight-day journey of Mary and Joseph from Nazareth to Bethlehem. For eight days they sought shelter, and on the ninth, Christmas Eve, they found lodging in a stable. There Christ was born and placed in a manger. While the background of the posada is deeply religious, the modern processions take on a festive atmosphere; they are held each night for nine nights, and invariably end with a party at which a *piñata* (pee-nyah′-tah), or hanging pot full of gifts, or candies and fruit, is broken. The procession consists of villagers, each carrying a lighted candle, and the *nacimiento,* (nah-see-myen′-toh) or "nativity scene," usually carried on a wagon pulled by young children. In the nacimiento are figurines (usually of clay) or Mary, Joseph, shepherds, animals, and the Three Wise Men. The marchers

(85)

go from house to house, singing traditional songs begging for *posada* or "lodging." Those on the outside sing one verse asking for help, and they are answered in song from those inside, telling them to go on their way. After many houses and many tries, finally someone inside sings that he does recognize the Holy Family and will let them in to rest. In many villages, it is considered the greatest honor of the year to have the posada procession enter one's home. Singing happily, the pilgrims rush inside, and all kneel briefly before the nacimiento. Then the party begins. Refreshments are served, and the piñata is brought out. The piñata originated in Italy during the Renaissance, when it was used for entertainment at masquerade balls. From Italy, the custom spread to Spain, and from there to Mexico. The piñata is a clay jug filled with candies or gifts and covered with papier-mâché and fringed colored paper. Shaped into fanciful animals, balls, or stars, the piñata is hung from a beam or hook in the ceiling; children are blindfolded and take turns trying to break it with a stick. Someone holds the rope attaching the piñata to the hook, and he pulls it up or down making it more difficult to hit. There is great excitement when finally the piñata shatters and everyone scrambles for the goodies that fall to the floor. The last piñata of the Christmas season is broken on Christmas Eve, in Spanish, *Noche Buena* (noh'-tshay bway-'nah) or "Good Night", at the party after Midnight Mass and the traditional feast. Earlier in the evening, the last posada was held. This differed from the others because for the first time, the figure of the Christ Child was placed in the nacimiento's manger, and Christ's birth was celebrated in song.

DONKEY PIÑATA

Materials: Poster paper or bristol board, two packages brightly colored crepe paper (single thickness), four double sheets newspaper (eight sides, standard folded daily-paper size—15″ by 23″), masking and cellophane tape, rubber cement, scissors, pencil, stapler, colored construction paper (contrast color to crepe paper), string or thin wire, hook (from which to hang piñata), stick (for knocking piñata), blindfold (handkerchief), wrapped candies, miniature favors, tiny gifts, etc. (for stuffing piñata), four cardboard tubes 5″ long.

1. Cut poster paper or bristol board into rectangle 12″ by 18″. To make donkey body, roll rectangle into a tube as shown, overlapping ends about 2″. Tape across center to hold and staple ends together.

2. Stand body tube on one end, over a second piece of poster paper (or bristol board) about 7″ by 12″. Draw around tube end. Repeat. Cut out two circles.

3. Roll four folded newspapers into a tube about 2½″ thick, as shown. Tape sides and ends firmly. Bend first 5″ or 6″ down from one end, making head and neck as shown.

4. Cut poster paper strip 2″ wide, 12″ long, to form ears. Cut ends of strip into points, as shown.

5. Cut one 3″-wide strip from folded package of crepe paper. Strip should be at least 50″ long. Unravel and fold strip in half lengthwise. Cut folded strip into fringe (see step 12). Wrap fringed paper around entire ear strip, overlapping edges. Tuck ends in and glue.

6. Tape ear strip into place under chin as shown (ears pointing up). Cross tape on cheeks to hold ears in place. *Note:* From here on, it is important to always use enough tape to anchor each part firmly in place. Tape will ultimately be covered with crepe paper, so use freely.

7. With seam of body tube down, mark top of one end where neck should go. Cut a small half-circle out at this point to fit in newspaper roll-neck (a).

(87)

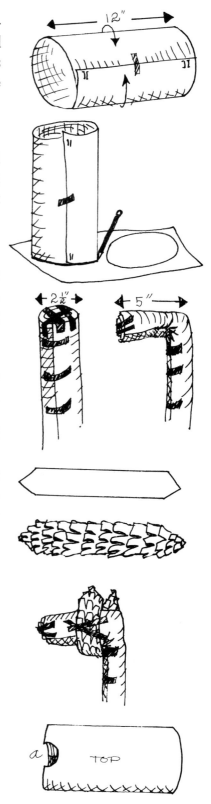

NOTE: Enlarge hole until neck fits exactly, as shown (b).

8. While holding head in this position, tape neck in place on body: begin with a 14″-long strip of masking tape, bring it around front of neck and cross ends on top of back (a). Next, lie donkey on side. Cut 8″-strip tape and press onto front of neck base, then around onto bottom of body tube (b-1). Cut two more 8″-tapes. Press one end of one onto left side of neck base then across neck front, fastening other end on *right* side of body tube (b-2). Repeat, pressing second tape onto right side of neck base, then across onto *left* side of tube (b-3).

9. After neck is firmly taped in place, tape one cardboard circle (step 2) over neck opening, as shown.

10. Take the four cardboard tubes, cut *one* end of each into ½″-long fringe as shown (a). Bend fringed edges back (b).

11. Mark four leg positions on underside of body tube. With body lying on side, press fringe-end of each leg down on mark and tape fringes flat to body.

12. Cut both folded packages of crepe paper into 3″-wide strips (a). Unravel and fold each strip in half lengthwise, giving a strip 1½″ wide. Cut folded strip into fringe as shown (b), cutting on fold side and leaving at least ¼″ uncut at base. Fringes will wind around and cover entire piñata.

13. Brush both cardboard circles (steps 2 and 9) with rubber cement. Cover with overlapping strips of fringe as shown. Trim and glue down edges. After piñata is filled, unattached circle will make a trap door on back end of donkey.

(88)

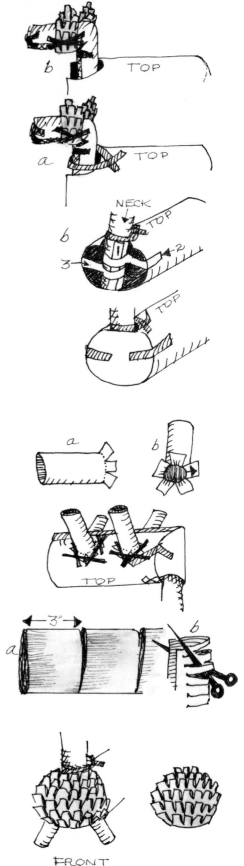

14. Cut out and glue on a flat circle of crepe paper over *end* of donkey's nose (a). Tape edges down if necessary to hold firmly. Spread rubber cement on sides of face. Begin winding on fringe, *loops toward nose* (b). *Note:* Overlap layers of fringe as they go on. When you reach end of one strip, glue (or cellophane tape) end down, cut another strip of fringe, and continue where you left off. Glue short strips of fringe between ears and wherever else there is not room to wind fringe. Cover entire body.

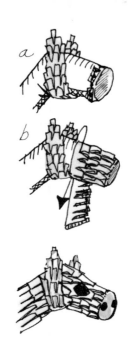

15. Cut out two contrasting colored construction paper eyes and glue over fringe on face. Also cut out two small circles for nostrils and glue onto flat of nose.

16. Fill open end of donkey with candies, favors, etc. Place fringe-covered circle over end, fasten in place *lightly* with two pieces of cellophane tape. When piñata is struck, this cover should easily fall open, spilling goodies out.

17. Tie thin wire or string around body as shown: bring string under belly behind front legs, forward to cross in *front* of neck, then back and tie *behind* neck. Leave end about 36″ long, then cut.

18. Tie a second string around middle of body, knot, and leave end 36″ long. Now hold up both strings, move mid-body string backward or forward until piñata is balanced and hangs horizontally. Tie strings together firmly, hang piñata from hook. Blindfold each player in turn, as he attempts to strike piñata with stick. Raise or lower piñata if you want to make the job more difficult.

NOTE: The same basic donkey figure may be made using a large oatmeal or corn-meal box for the body. Cut holes in box to insert tubes for neck and legs, finish as above. Cut out box bottom, then tape it on lightly for trap door.

(89)

Chanukah

The most important winter festival of the Jewish religion is *Chanukah* (hah'-nu-kah). Derived from the Hebrew word meaning "dedication," Chanukah is the "Feast of Dedication," also known as the "Festival of Lights." It is celebrated for eight days, beginning on the twenty-fifth day of the Hebrew month Kislev (November-December). The holiday honors an event which took place over two thousand years ago, when a small band of heroic Jewish men fought a victorious battle for religious freedom.

In the second century before Christ, Palestine was under Syrian-Greek rule led by King Antiochus Epiphanes. Antiochus, sometimes called "the madman," was determined to bring all his subjects under the Greek religion. But the Jews refused to submit to him, and in the village of Modin, near Jerusalem, a priest known as Mattathias, and his five sons, began a rebellion. Under the leadership of one of the sons, Judas Maccabeus ("the Hammerer"), the small band of "Maccabees" fought hard. The soldiers of Antiochus had overrun the Jewish temple and dedicated it to Greek gods; but finally, the Maccabees were successful in driving them out and bringing peace to the land.

On the twenty-fifth day of Kislev, in the year 165 B.C., the Maccabees entered the temple which the Greeks had taken over. They needed oil to rededicate the temple and to light the holy candelabra, the *menorah*. A very tiny container of oil was found, and while it did not seem to be enough to last for even one day, the menorah is said to have continued to burn for eight days. For this reason, Chanukah is known as the "Festival of Lights."

Chanukah is now celebrated in Jewish homes by the lighting of a small menorah with special candles, and the reciting of blessings of thanks to God. The first candle is lit at sundown on the evening of the twenty-fourth of Kislev when the holiday begins. An extra candle, called the *shammesh*, or "servant," is also lit each night and then used to light the other candles. On the second night, two candles are lit, in addition to the shammesh; on each night thereafter, one more candle is added until on the eighth night, eight candles and the shammesh are burning together.

In Israel, menorahs are lit everywhere. The city of Tel Aviv is called the "City of Lights" at this time, because all the lights of the city are left on during the nights of Chanukah. Every public building displays its own menorah, illuminating an additional candle each night as one does in the home. This is an especially gay holiday for children, who hold Chanukah parties, sing songs, play *dreidle* (dray'-del), or "top," games and eat potato pancakes, called *latkes*. Latkes are as traditional for Chanukah as regular pancakes are for the Christian holiday of Shrove Tuesday (see page 138).

After lighting the menorah, games are played and gifts exchanged during *each* Chanukah evening. It is traditional for children to receive, among other things, little gifts of money, called *Chanukah gelt* on each of the eight nights. Dreidle games are enjoyed by everyone in the family. The dreidle was used even in ancient times, and in places where Jews were forbidden to practice their religion, they often met to play the dreidle while they secretly prayed together. There are four Hebrew letters on the dreidle: Nun, Gimel, Hay, Shin. Taken together, the letters NGHS stand for the words *nes gadol hayeh sham*, meaning "a great miracle happened there," referring to the oil that lasted for eight days. Hebrew letters also have number values, and nun equals 50, gimel —3, hay—5, and shin—300. "Put and take" games are played with the dreidle using these numbers.

DREIDLE *(Top)*

Materials: Cardboard or construction paper, cotton swab or lollypop stick, scissors, crayons or felt pens, rubber cement.

1. Cut 2″-square of cardboard or construction paper (see page 20, Method I).

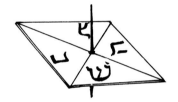

2. Decorate as shown, drawing diagonal lines with the help of a ruler. Then, in each section, draw the Hebrew letters as shown: נ —Nun, ג —Gimmel, ה —Hay, ש —Shin.

3. Insert lollypop stick or cotton swab stick (cotton removed) in center of crossed lines. Brush a drop of glue over hole to hold stick in place. For dreidle to spin correctly, *be sure stick is perpendicular to paper.*

1. Each player in turn spins the dreidle, and wins the number of points corresponding to the Hebrew letter which lands upright (see above). Highest total score wins.

2. The letters on the dreidle are also the initials of Yiddish words. Nun stands for *nichts*, meaning "nothing"; gimmel for *gantz*, meaning "all"; hay for *halb*, meaning "half"; and shin for *shtell*, meaning "put in" or "add." Each player puts several tokens (dry beans, chips, etc.) in a central pot. Then each in turn spins the dreidle and, depending upon which letter comes up, they either add to, get nothing, half, or all the tokens in the pot. Player getting most tokens wins.

New Year's Day

Signs of nature such as changing seasons, stars, moons, bird migrations, water tides, and annual floods showed ancient men when to celebrate their New Year. For example, Egypt in the year 4241 B.C., celebrated the New Year at the time of the Nile River's flood, on July 19. The ancient countries including the Mesopotamian areas of Babylonia, Sumer, and Palestine divided the year into two parts, observing one New Year in the autumn at the end of summer's heat, and a second New Year at the end of winter's cold, during the warm early spring rains when the first crops appeared. Romans before Julius Caesar generally celebrated in March, the first month of their year. After the year 46 B.C., Caesar's reformed "Julian" calendar changed the New Year celebration to January 1. Pope Gregory XIII, in 1582, further changed the calendar and confirmed the January 1 New Year, though many countries continued to hold on to their spring New Year festivities (see page 149). The Romans had named the first month of their new year cycle (Januarius) for the god Janus, Keeper of Doors and Gates. Janus is shown with two faces, one looking back to the past, the other looking forward to the future. He symbolized beginnings and endings, and always held a scepter, the symbol of power, and a key with which to close the old year's door and open the one to the new.

The custom of gift-giving on New Year's Day originated, as did so many of our customs, with the ancient Romans, who made gifts an important part of their end-of-year Saturnalia festival. In addition, on New Year's Day they exchanged gifts of coins bearing the portrait of the god Janus. In England, New Year gift-giving became especially popular during the sixteenth century, when favorite gifts were pomander balls, gilded nutmegs, and fine leather gloves. During the reign of Henry VIII, a new and exquisite luxury was devised for ladies' gifts: decorative metal pins. Previously, pins were carved from bone or wood in skewer fashion, and no woman of elegance could have too many of the new designs. Money spent for these gifts was called "pin money."

JANUS PIN

Janus pins, decorated with the Roman New Year god's portrait, may be made at a New Year's Eve party at home or in school, with each member of the group decorating his own pin. Or, they may be made in advance and given to friends as favors or gifts on the holiday.

Materials: Clean, wide-mouthed tin can (#3 or larger), water, plaster of paris (see page 17), wax paper, tempera paint, brush, emery board or *fine* sandpaper, Elmer's or Sobo glue, pencil, white shellac, alcohol (solvent for shellac), shellac brush, measuring cups, pin backs, newspapers.

1. Spread newspapers over work area. Pour ½ cup water into can. Slowly sprinkle about ¾ cup plaster of paris *on top of water,* mixing with your hands. Squish plaster and water together; continue adding plaster until mixture is as thick as *soft* ice cream.

2. Spread wax paper. Drop about a tablespoon of plaster from your hand onto wax paper as shown. Shape in round, oval, or irregular forms, about 1½″ to 2″ across. Smooth peak as much as possible with finger.

3. You will have enough plaster for about 20 shapes. Let them sit until hard, at least 40 minutes.

4. Flattest side of shapes will hold pin back. To smooth front, remove any lumps or jagged edges first with rough, then smooth side of emery board (or sandpaper). Round edges as shown. *Note:* Shape may be left jagged and lumpy if you prefer.

(93)

5. With pencil, sketch design *lightly* on front of plaster shape. Paint design with tempera paint. Wait about 10 minutes, until paint is completely dry.

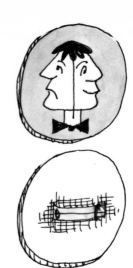

6. Shellac painted front, and sides, of shape; set on wax paper to dry (about 15 minutes). When dry, turn piece over, shellac back and dry.

7. Glue pin onto back; let glue dry thoroughly before wearing pin.

In the United States, gifts are rarely exchanged on New Year's Day, though sometimes holiday foods are brought to one's host when making traditional New Year visits. In other countries, New Year gift-giving is much more common. In Italy, children receive little money gifts, called *strenna* (stray'-nah), and in Rome, Italians pile gifts upon the platforms of the traffic policemen in the streets. In Greece, St. Basil is said to come, bringing toys to fill the shoes of the children, who are awakened at midnight to toast the New Year with the adults while opening their gifts. In France, friends and relatives exchange New Year gifts, *les étrennes* (laiz-ay-tren'), and at the stroke of midnight, kiss one another under the mistletoe.

Many New Year's customs had their origins in Scotland and England. "First Footing," for example, dates from earliest Scottish history. The tradition is still observed, whereby the family's fortune in the New Year is determined by whomever is the first guest to set foot (first footer) in the door after the New Year strikes. It is extremely bad luck for the first footer to be a woman, a light-haired man, an undertaker, or anyone who walks with his toes pointing inward. A dark-haired man, however, brings good luck. In many villages, such men hire out as professional first footers, whose job it is to go from house to house immediately after the New Year arrives.

When the dark man enters the house as a first footer, he must bring a *handsel,* some piece of bread, salt, orange, or corn carried in the hand for good luck. Good luck only comes if something is carried *into* the house on the New Year; it is bad luck to carry anything out. Sometimes the first footer brings cheese or cakes which he shares with the family. This is perhaps the origin of our custom of sharing holiday foods on New Year's Day visits. *Hogmanay* is the Scottish name for New Year's Eve, and one of the foods traditionally shared with the first footer is Hogmanay Shortbread, baked in a special "sun" shape, a survival of pagan sun worship.

SCOTTISH HOGMANAY SHORTBREAD

Ingredients: 1 cup sweet butter (leave out of refrigerator until soft)
                ½ cup confectioners' sugar
                2 cups sifted flour

Equipment: Mixing bowl, ungreased cookie sheet, fork, table knife, sifter, apron, ruler or tape measure, spatula.

1. Preheat oven to 325°.

2. Wash hands thoroughly before mixing and handling dough. Mix butter and sugar together, either with fork or hands.

3. Sift in flour, mixing dough with hands until *just* blended. To keep dough tender and crisp, it should *not* be over handled. Shape dough into a ball, remove from bowl, and set upon an ungreased cookie sheet.

4. With hands, press (do not roll) dough into a flat round cake, about ¾″ thick and 8″ across.

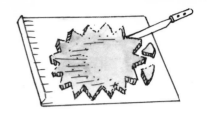

5. Notch edges of cake with knife, cutting out small triangles around edge as shown, giving shortcake the traditional sun shape of Hogmanay.

6. Divide the sun with a fork into eight equal wedges by pricking along dotted lines as shown. After baking, this will make shortcake easier to serve.

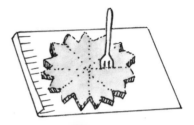

7. Bake shortcake at 325° for about 45 minutes, until golden. When cool, move to a plate with spatula. Store shortcake in airtight container. Warm in oven to recrisp, if necessary.

After the first footing at midnight on Hogmanay, families visit back and forth sharing their shortbreads and drinking "wassail," a spiced ale punch whose name comes from the Old English *wæs hæil, meaning* "to your health."

WASSAIL

According to an old custom, the New Year wassail bowl often became a fortune-teller. In England, for example, the wassail (or posset pot as it was called in some countries) contained a ring, and each unmarried guest at the New Year's Eve party tried to catch the ring in his ladle full of punch. If he was successful, he would marry during that year. For your New Year's Eve party, prepare a wassail bowl (or posset pot) of mixed fruit punch (lemon or orange-ade, pineapple juice, and ginger ale). Add red and green maraschino cherries and orange and lemon slices to the punch. Allow each guest to ladle his own cup of wassail-fortune: A red cherry means wealth during the year, green means happiness, an orange slice means a surprise, and a lemon slice means something unpleasant.

Since ancient times, it has been the custom, virtually around the world, to make loud noises during the first minutes of the New Year. This was intended to frighten away any evil spirits who might be lurking, waiting to spoil the New Year. Today, we see this tradition in our New Year's Eve party noise-makers, in the old crockery which in Italy is thrown from windows crashing down into the streets on New Year's Eve, and in the church bells everywhere that ring in the New Year. In England, church bells are often covered with cloth to muffle the sound during the last few minutes of the old year. At the stroke of midnight, the cloth is removed, and the bells loudly peal in the New Year.

The *good-luck pig* is a popular New Year tradition in Austria. The pig has always been a symbol of good luck for the Indo-European peoples. It has been said that this is because a pig digs in a forward direction, thus being a symbol of a "fat future." Whatever the reason, the popularity of the fat good-luck pig survives in our "piggy" banks, in the form of a candy-pig Christmas tree decoration popular in Europe, in the eating of roast pork on feast days as is the custom in many parts of Europe, and in the traditional New Year pig. In Austria, he can be made of wood, cookies, clay, or marzipan, and has either a gold coin or a four-leaf clover in his mouth. The little pink pig, in any or all of these forms, is given as a good-luck gift on New Year's Day.

MARZIPAN

Ingredients: 8 oz. can (1 cup) almond paste
1¾ cups confectioners' sugar
1 egg white
2 teaspoons almond extract
vegetable food coloring
cocoa

Equipment: Large mixing bowl, apron, table knife, wax paper, pencil, colored toothpicks, colored paper (or ready-made miniature stems and leaves, found in party supply shops), scissors, black stiff paper, small new paint brush (optional).

1. Separate egg, and place white in mixing bowl. Add almond paste. Mix the ingredients together with your hands (be sure to wash hands first).

2. When well blended, add almond extract and sugar. Work with hands until dough is well blended and stiff enough to shape. If possible, let dough sit an hour or so before shaping to "ripen."

3. Shape dough into a ball, turn onto pastry board or clean counter sprinkled with confectioners' sugar. Sugar hands while shaping dough. Add more sugar to dough as needed to make stiff enough to model. Knead dough several times before shaping, as directed below.

NOTE: Recipe makes about 24 pieces, depending upon size. Wrapped airtight in foil or plastic wrap, marzipan keeps several weeks.

SHAPING MARZIPAN

PIG

1. Pull off lump of dough for pig. Add two or three drops of red food coloring to dough, work in until evenly colored pink.

2. Shape fat, stubby roll of dough for body.

3. Add two similar rolls to underside for legs. Pinch in place as with clay.

4. Stand pig up, pinch up ears, shape face and neck as shown.

5. With knife, cut in mouth as shown.

6. Dip toothpick in green coloring, make two dots for eyes, two for nostrils. Draw tail curl on back end.

7. With silver or gold tinfoil, cover a small coin, or cut green paper 4-leaf clover, place in pig's mouth. Stand him on wax paper to dry.

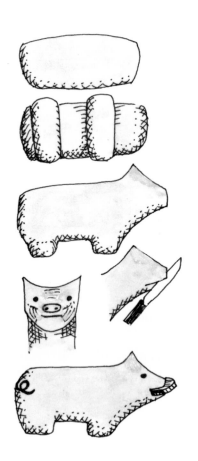

(98)

FRUIT

1. Pull off small lumps of dough, form as shown, into strawberry, peach, apple, lemon, banana, etc. Set shapes on wax paper.

2. To color, squirt several drops of needed colors into small glasses or cups, or paper baking cups. Add a few drops of water to lighten each color. Dip new paint brush or finger into color and spread over shape. If a second color is to be used, wait until first is dry before adding. For strawberry dots, dip end of toothpick in green, poke into dry red strawberry. Dab green on ends of yellow banana.

3. Use half green toothpick for stems, cut out paper or foil leaves, or use ready-made stems.

BAKED POTATO

1. Pull off small lump of dough, roll into oval ball.

2. Roll ball in cocoa spread on wax paper.

3. With knife, slit cross in top of potato (a), and pinch to open cross (b). Set on wax paper to dry.

a   b

(99)

LADYBUG

1. Pull off lump of dough and shape into ball about 1½″ across. Flatten into half-ball as shown.

2. Set shape on piece of black paper, draw with pencil around edge of body (a). Then remove dough to wax paper and draw ladybug's antennae and legs as shown (b). Cut shape out.

a

3. Brush or rub red food coloring over half-ball of dough. Let dry, thoroughly.

b

4. Add green coloring as shown, using new brush or toothpick to make head, back line, and spots.

5. Mix tablespoon of confectioners' sugar with few drops of water to make *thick* paste. Place this "glue" in center of cutout black paper and press body down onto it. Be sure body is firmly set on paper and only antennae and legs show.

(100)

Noruz

In Iran, Moslems and non-Moslems alike celebrate *Noruz* (No-rooz), literally "New Day" or the New Year, which, unlike the Western European day, begins on the twenty-first of March and lasts for thirteen days. At the start of the holiday, homes are thoroughly cleaned, and children given new clothes and presents. The evening before Noruz begins, a traditional omelette made with greens is eaten with pilaf, the national dish of rice symbolizing an abundant year. Friends visit and exchange gifts such as colored eggs, fruits, and bunches of narcissus.

A special festival table is prepared for Noruz, on which are the *Haft-Sin*, or "Seven S's." These seven items beginning with the letter "s" represent the seven archangels of God, who embody the abstractions of ethical behavior in the Zoroastrian religion of Iran. The objects, chosen to represent happiness in the New Year, are: *sabzeh*—green sprouts grown from seed, *sonbul*—hyacinth, *samanoo*—sweet wheat pudding, *serkeh*—vinegar, *sumac*—same as our sumac plant, *seeb*—apple, *senjed*—Bohemian olives. Besides the Haft-Sin, there are eggs colored like our Easter eggs (symbolizing new life), a candle for each member of the family and a mirror (to reflect one's bright future), green leaves, roast chicken, fruits, bread, sweets (for a sweet life), and rose water. After the feast, sweet candy is passed while a passage of the Koran (the Moslem holy book) is read.

About fifteen days before the holiday, each family begins to grow the traditional *sabzeh*—grains of wheat, lentils, or barley germinated in a dish or clay jug moistened with water. The sabzeh slowly grow up until, by Noruz, they are a mass of greens, symbolizing life and good fortune.

On the thirteenth day of Noruz, called *Sizdan-Bedar,* or "Thirteenth Day Out," it is considered unlucky to remain at home; the entire family goes to the country to spend the day and to welcome the spring. One also leaves behind all the bad luck associated with the number thirteen. While picnic lunches are eaten, folk singers, dancers, clowns, and costumed actors wander about the countryside amusing and entertaining the people. The sabzeh have been brought from home, and at this time are carefully thrown into a stream, or some running water, to symbolize the throwing away of all bad luck, family quarrels, and illness. Thus, the New Year can begin in peace and friendship.

SABZEH

Materials: Shallow bowl or pie plate, clear plastic bag large enough to cover plate, desk blotter or cheesecloth, water, dry beans (red kidney, lentils, navy, etc.) or grass seed.

1. Cut two or three pieces of blotter to cover the bottom of plate, or fold triple thickness of cheesecloth.

2. Set blotter or cloth in bottom of plate, add enough water to dampen well. Pour off extra water. Sprinkle seeds or beans on top of moistened surface. Seeds or beans may be placed close together, as shown.

3. Slip plate inside plastic bag, wire or tie end closed, and set by the window. Check each day to be sure blotter or cloth is always damp, providing moisture the seeds need in order to germinate or sprout. From time to time, gently tap the top of plastic bag causing condensed water droplets to fall back onto seeds. If bag is airtight, you will need to add *very little extra water. Do not add too much water,* or seeds or beans will rot. If mildew begins, remove plate from bag until excess moisture has evaporated.

4. After about seven days, depending upon the type of bean or seed, the first tendrils of root will begin to appear (a). Then stems will raise up and in about two weeks you will have shoots with leaves (b).

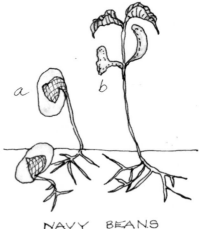

NAVY BEANS

Oshoogatsu

In Japan, the New Year, called *Oshoogatsu* (oh-show-gah-tsu), is officially celebrated on January 1. As in almost every country in the world, housecleaning is important and must be completed before New Year's Eve. No sweeping is allowed on New Year's Day, lest the good spirits of the New Year be accidentally swept away. The entrance to one's home is scrubbed to welcome the New Year, and special decorations are placed on the front of the house. Beside the front door, pine branches and bamboo stalks are hung, symbolizing long life and virtue. Ropes of braided rice straw, called *shimenawa* (shi-men-nah-wah), are hung on house fronts and gates to bring good luck and keep out evil. In addition, a decoration unique to the New Year, called *shimekazari* (shi-meh-kah-zah-ree), is hung over the door. It consists of a long brushlike arrangement of straw, to which objects signifying happiness and good luck are attached. These include seaweed, ferns, a red and white paper fan on which is written the Japanese character meaning "to celebrate happy events," and an orange or lobster section. Hanging down are red and white paper *gohei* (goh-hay), the folded four-squared traditional paper decoration bringing good luck. To celebrate the New Year's Eve, adults stay up to hear a special gong ring one hundred and eight times, symbolically cleansing the one hundred and eight human weaknesses described in the teachings of Buddha. Children receive New Year's gifts, often wear new clothes, and at the New Year feast, the family shares the traditionally festive rice cakes.

SHIMEKAZARI

Materials: Straw twine (¼″ thick) or straw or straw-colored raffia, flexible thin wire, scissors, ruler, pencil, red paper, tangerine or mandarin orange or orange colored paper, ferns or green colored paper, seaweed (optional), black felt pen, darning needle, carpet thread, masking tape.

1. To make braid of twine or straw, cut three (or six if twine is thin) pieces of twine 20″ long; or three bunches (several strands each) of raffia or straw same length, and one piece of wire 20″ long.

2. Gather the braiding material and wire together and tie a knot, as shown, about 1½″ from one end.

3. Keeping the wire with one of the three strands or bunches, braid to within 2″ of end, tie knot as shown above, and curve braid into a "U" shape.

4. Cut about 30 strands of raffia, straw, or thin straw twine 24″ long. Place strands flat on table, ends even. Place curved braid *under* strands, about 3″ down from one end. Center the braid, and slip a piece of wire or thread under it, bringing ends up and tying them over straw strands, fixing them to center of braid as shown.

5. To make fan, cut rectangle of red paper 6″ by 3½″. With paper in position shown, copy Japanese character "Kotobuki" meaning "to celebrate happy events" in center with felt pen.

TOP

6. To fold fan:

   a. With short end on bottom as shown, fold bottom edge up about ½″ and press on fold.

   b. Turn piece face down, folded edge on top. Bend folded edge back ½″ and down onto what is now front side, as shown. Press on fold.

   c. Turn piece face up, and fold as in step (a). Keep all folds same width. Repeat steps (a), (b), and (c) until all paper is folded.

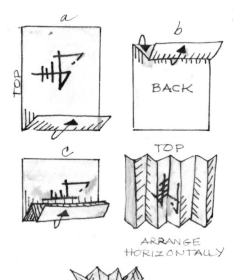

7. Fold fan together, pinch one end, and wrap masking tape around bottom ½″ to hold base, as shown.

8. If you have a tangerine or orange, push a wire through it and tie onto center of braided curve as shown (a). Thread darning needle with carpet thread, stitch through sides of fan base (b). Directly behind orange, sew fan (face forward), onto back of braided curve. Seen from the front, top of fan should stick up above orange. *Note:* If you do not have real orange, make one from paper. Cut a 2″ square of orange paper and trim into circle (see page 20, Method I).

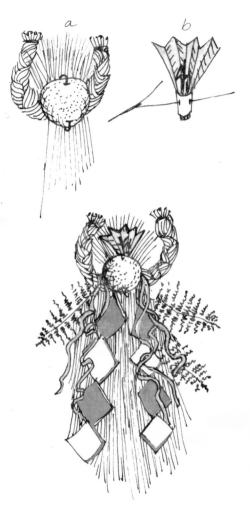

9. If you have seaweed, tie thread onto one end of each of several pieces and then tie them onto braid, so they hang below orange. To "make" your own seaweed, cut narrow strips of green paper ½″ wide by 18″ long or paint raffia green. Tie these onto braid.

10. Tie three or four ferns onto braid with thread as shown, or draw ferns on green paper about 12″ long, and cut them out. Thread needle with carpet thread, stitch into stem of paper fern, remove needle, and tie thread onto braid.

11. Finally, tie *Gohei* (see below) onto braid as shown and hang your shimekazari over the door on the New Year.

GOHEI

Gohei are sometimes made from single strips of white paper, but on special occasions such as the New Year, they are made of red and white, the traditional colors of happiness and congratulations. Gifts are also wrapped in red and white paper.

Materials: Red and white paper, pencil, ruler, scissors, darning needle, carpet thread.

(105)

1. Cut two strips of paper, one red, one white, 12″ long, 3½″ wide.

2. On white piece, measure, mark, and draw a light pencil line across, ½″ in from long edges.

3. Divide the length of paper into 3″ sections. Draw cutting lines as shown: first draw in from *right* edge and stop at left margin; second, draw in from *left* edge and stop at right margin; third, like first.

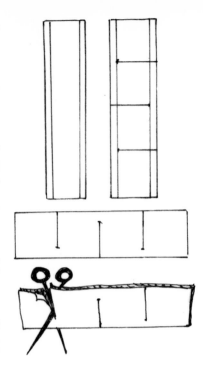

4. Erase side margin lines, leaving only cutting lines.

5. Place white strip on top of red. Holding strips together, line up edges and cut along cutting lines.

6. To fold:

   a. Place cut strips together, white up, flat on table. Fold top section over to the *left,* making a fold where the margin line was. Red side of that section is now facing up.

   b. Holding first red section down as shown, fold *third* section over to the *right,* red side up.

   c. Now fold last section over to *right,* so its white side is up, as shown.

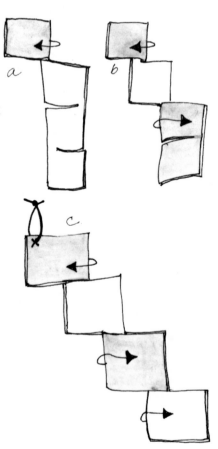

7. Thread darning needle with carpet thread that is knotted in one end (see page 19). Holding folded strips together, stitch through "X" in corner of top section (see step 6 (c)). Pull thread through until knot holds on one side, remove needle, tie thread onto shimekazari (above).

Yuan Tan

The Chinese New Year, *Yuan Tan* (wahn-tahn) is celebrated on the first day of the month in the lunar calendar (between January 21 and February 19). The New Year is a particularly gay holiday, for it is generally the day on which people celebrate their birthdays, although now some prefer the Western method of observing the actual date of birth. It is a family holiday, enjoyed especially by children.

The first few days are treated very carefully, so nothing will be done to spoil the entrance of the New Year or cause bad luck. Meatless meals are prepared, offerings of incense are made to household gods, debts are settled (before New Year's Eve), quarrels are forgiven, and swearing is forbidden. New clothes are worn, and gifts are given to children. These are primarily coins wrapped in red paper, called *ya sway chien*, or "press the year money," meaning "to push down the old year." Some lucky children receive the red-wrapped coins from adults the first time they are seen every day for six to ten days. The celebration in the home lasts about ten days, with great banquets, and friends visiting one another bringing gifts of nuts, watermelon seeds, and fine teas. Red paper decorations with good-luck phrases written on them hang over doors, windows, and gates to ward off bad luck. Red candles are burned for good luck, and special flowers are used to decorate the home: white narcissus (for good luck), peach or plum (for long life), any red blossoms (for good luck and happiness), and peonies (for wealth). If a blossom opens on New Year's Day, it is a sign of an especially good future.

The most exciting event of the holiday takes place on the night of the full moon, called *Yuan Shaw*. A special candy, called *yuan shaw* is eaten on this day, made of a sweet nut mixture rolled in rice flour. Yuan Shaw is "The Festival of the Lanterns," and elaborate lanterns are made in every shape— balls, boxes, animals, airplanes—and carried on bamboo poles through the streets during the evening "Parade of the Dragon." The dragon, symbol of strength and goodness, has a fantastic papier-mâché or wooden head attached to a cloth and bamboo body; under the cloth, as many as fifty men walk and dance. The dragon's head is painted red, with gold and silver decorations all over the face, silver horns, and usually a green beard. Crowds gather to watch the parade, carrying their lanterns, and throwing firecrackers to make as much noise as possible and thus scare away any evil spirits, assuring good luck for the New Year.

(107)

DRAGON LANTERN

While the traditional New Year's dragon is an elaborate construction, a simplified version may be made in the form of an individual lantern with the dragon head made of folded paper fitted onto a flashlight, and the body a spike-spined arm sleeve.

Materials: Green (or other color) fabric or crepe paper for arm sleeve, white or colored paper for head, scissors, stapler, ruler, darning needle, carpet thread, flashlight.

1. To make dragon's head, cut 12″ square of paper (see page 20, Method II). Fold square in half. Mark light pencil 4 on outside, in bottom right corner as shown (a). Open paper, with 4 in bottom right as shown, and mark light pencil 3 in upper left corner (b).

2. Turn paper over (so 3 is *under* bottom left corner) and mark light pencil 1 in upper left corner, and 2 in lower right corner as shown (a). Then fold in half the opposite way, with 4 in upper left corner (b).

3. Open again, fold along diagonal as shown, with 4 in upper right.

4. Open, and *with 4 on inside,* fold along opposite diagonal so 4 faces 3.

5. Now open square, place flat on table in position shown (a), *with 4 on underside* at top corner. Bring points 1 and 2 *up and in toward the center,* as shown (b).

(108)

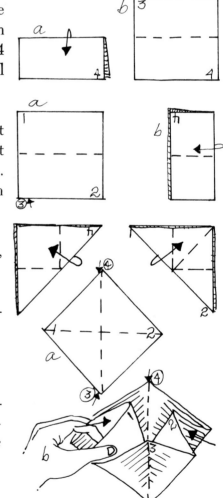

6. Bring points 1 and 2 together until their folds meet. Bring points 3 and 4 up to meet points 1 and 2. Press folded square flat along arrows.

7. Fold point 3 over in half as shown, exposing points 1 and 2. Press along fold.

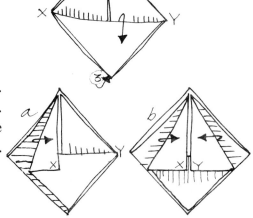

8. Fold point X over to the center, as shown. Line its outside edge up with center fold (a). Repeat with point Y, bringing its outside edge over to meet in center with that of point X (b).

9. Fold point 3 *up*, covering bottoms of the last two folds, as shown.

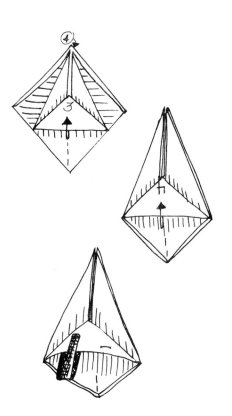

10. Turn piece over, *keeping point 4 on top,* and repeat steps 7, 8, and 9. *Note:* This time, remember, you are working with point 4, not 3. Shape now looks like this.

11. Slip stapler inside "pockets" as shown, and staple flaps, on both sides, to folded-over sections. This will hold head firmly in shape.

12. Before opening dragon head, decorate with eyes and rows of teeth on each side. Top and bottom of head may also be decorated, with felt pens or crayons.

13. To make hole for flashlight, cut about 1″ (for standard-size flashlight, less for smaller sizes) off tips of back folds as shown.

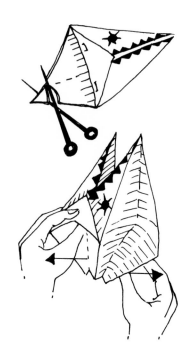

14. To open head, place thumbs inside "pockets" on each side and gently pull out as shown. Pull out until head stays open by itself.

15. Open dragon head looks like this: front view (a), side view (b).

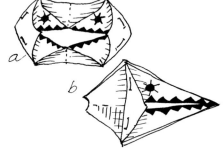

16. Fit bulb end of flashlight inside hole (which should be enlarged if necessary until correct size). Tape as shown, firmly attaching head to handle.

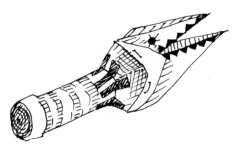

(110)

17. To make sleeve, measure length of your arm (armpit to fingertips); cut fabric or crepe paper to this length and 14″ or more in width.

18. Fold piece in half lengthwise and hem about ½″ inside opened edges as shown. Staple hem (a) or sew with darning needle and carpet thread (b).

19. To make spine-spikes, cut ten (more if needed) construction paper triangles about 2″ wide at base, 2″ high.

20. With sleeve flat on table, *hemmed edge up*, staple base of each triangle to top of sleeve, as shown. *Note:* Place staples not more than ½″ in from top.

21. To assemble dragon, slide sleeve over your arm, spikes up. Hold flashlight handle in hand inside sleeve, so only dragon head sticks out. On the night of Yuan Shaw, light your flashlight, wiggle your sleeved arm, and add your illuminated dragon to the New Year parade.

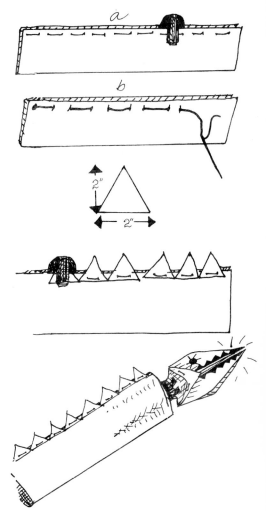

DRAGON MASK

The dragon head may also be made into a head mask. Use a 30″ square of paper (approximately 36″ for adults, 24″ for up to eight years old), fold and decorate as above, up to step 12. Open as in step 14. Cut a small hole in center of widest part of bottom, as shown. Keep fitting and enlarging hole until it fits over your head. Press strips of masking tape over edges of hole to keep them from tearing. Wear your dragon mask in the New Year parade or on Halloween.

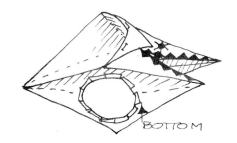

(111)

Epiphany

The sixth of January is a holiday with three names: Epiphany, Three Kings' Day, and Twelfth Night. This date has been a holiday in Eastern countries since the ancient Egyptians celebrated their winter solstice festival in honor of the Nile River. On this day, the river water was believed to be purest, and so was drawn and stored in special containers for use on holy occasions throughout the year. With the arrival of Christianity in Egypt, the day became a celebration of the baptism of Christ in the River Jordan. Holy water was still drawn on this day, but used for the year's baptisms and sacraments. Observance of Christ's baptism on this date spread to the West in the fourth century, about the same time the date of his birth was fixed as the twenty-fifth of December and Christmas became an important festival (see page 72). In addition to celebrating the baptism on this day, Western Christians also celebrate the Miracle of Cana, when Christ is said to have turned water into wine, and Three Kings' Day, when the Kings, or *Magi,* brought gifts to the Christ Child in Bethlehem.

The Magi were a sect of priests in ancient Media in Persia. They were wise men, famous for their knowledge of the natural sciences, including astrology, astronomy (study of the stars), and enchantments. It is believed that our word "magic" comes from "Magi." The Magi carefully observed the stars, and on the night of Christ's birth, it is said that they noticed a star shining in the east more brilliantly than any star ever shone before. This, they clamed, was the "Star of Bethlehem," or "Star in the East," shining to show them the way to Christ. It has never been exactly determined which country the Magi came from, or how many there were on the trip to Bethlehem. An old tradition of the Oriental Church says there were twelve; however, the Western Church established the belief, which has come down to us, that there were three Magi, or "Kings" as they were called early in the Christian Era, representing three races of man.

Each King was said to have brought a symbolic gift to Christ. Balthasar, a bearded Negro, King of Ethiopia, carried frankincense, a gum used as incense, and a symbol of purification for a high priest. Melchior, an old man and King of Arabia (some believe he was a Hindu) brought a casket of gold, the wealth of the East, to the newborn King. Gaspar, the young, light-skinned King (possibly a Greek), carried myrrh, an incense and holy ointment, the symbol of a great physician.

In many countries, special ceremonies and festivities are held on January 6 in honor of the Three Magi. In Sweden, Austria, and Switzerland, for example, young people choose three among them to dress in costumes of the three Kings. Then, following the Kings, they form processions marching through the streets of the village singing special carols and carrying a large "Star of Bethlehem" as their banner. In many villages of Switzerland, children celebrate "Sternsingen" (shtern'-sing-en), or "Star Singing," with an elaborate pageant. Three are chosen to dress as the Kings. They march in a torchlight procession, bearing their gifts to the manger scene, where others portray members of the Holy Family. Around the manger stand "angels," wearing white robes and halos, holding a great illuminated "Star of Bethlehem" on a tall pole.

THREE KINGS' COSTUMES

Materials: Old sheets (single bed) or other fabric similar size, colored poster paper or 1-ply bristol board, crepe paper or fabric in assorted colors, stapler, ruler, scissors, tempera paint and brush or colored felt pens, crown decorations: old costume jewelry, colored foil, etc.

GOWN

1. Use half or whole sheet depending upon size of wearer. For whole sheet, cut 1'-wide strip off the side lengthwise. Cut hole in center of remaining large piece.

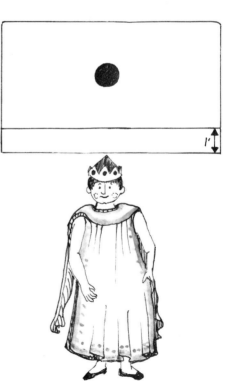

2. Decorate fabric with border designs of brightly colored tempera paint or felt pens.

3. To wear gown, drape sheet over body, lengthwise, head in hole. Drape narrow strip across front of neck, ends hanging down in back. Cut hem correct length.

CROWN I

1. Cut a circle 14″ across (see page 20, Method I—trimming a 14″ square, or III) of poster paper or bristol board. Cut out a 12″-long wedge as shown (a), then pull paper around into cone and measure on head. Overlap ends until it fits, staple to hold (b).

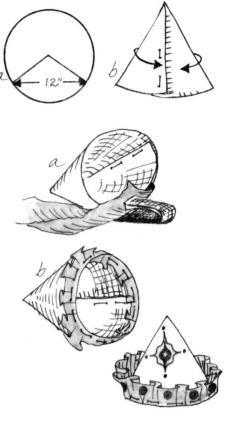

2. Cut strip of crepe paper 24″ long, 8″ wide. Fold in half lengthwise. Place folded strip on table, open edge toward you. Set cone over strip as shown, point away from you. Turn edges of strip inside cone about 1″ and staple to brim (a). Overlap crepe paper into folds as you staple, so it fits on cone. Try to keep staples at even distance from cone bottom (b).

3. Stand hat up as shown and decorate, glueing on costume jewelry, foil, etc. Spread paper border open.

CROWN II

1. Cut strip of poster paper or bristol board 21″ by 4″. Cut points along one side as shown (a). Pull ends around into circle, overlapping them until strip fits head. Staple ends to hold (b).

2. Cut crepe paper circle 12″ across (see page 20, Method I, II, or III). Fit crepe paper circle inside ring to form a liner. Overlap liner edges and staple to inside of ring as shown.

3. Stand crown up as shown and decorate.

CROWN III

1. Cut strip of poster paper or bristol board 21″ by 2″. Cut two strips 12″ by 1½″. Cut crepe paper circle 12″ across (see page 20, Method I, II, or III).

2. Wind longest strip around into circle, over-lapping ends until it fits on head. Staple to hold.

3. Staple on cross pieces as shown, ends on *in-side* of ring.

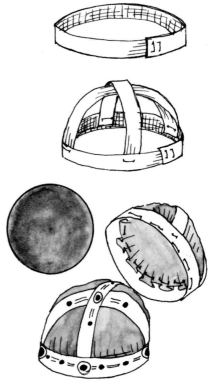

4. To make liner, spread crepe paper circle *in-side* crown; overlap liner edges into folds and staple to inside of ring. Puff out liner evenly.

5. Stand crown up as shown and decorate.

CHRIST CHILD'S GIFTS

Frankincense: Cover tall jar with tinfoil.
Gold: Paint box gold, paint or glue on colored costume jewelry.
Myrrh: Cover fat bottle (peanut butter jar) with tinfoil squeezed into little knobs all over surface; make fancy tinfoil top. Set all gifts on colored cushions, to be carried by Three Kings.

In Italy, Epiphany Eve, *La Vigilia dell'Epifania* (lah vee-geé-lya del-ae-peef-ahn-eé-ya), is the day of the *Befana*. The Befana is a kindly old lady, wearing a babushka and carrying a broom, who is said to bring gifts to good children and charcoal to bad children on this night, January 5. The Befana's name comes from the word *Epifania*, or "Epiphany," and her legend is very old.

The Befana lived long, long ago. Her husband and child had fallen ill and died, and she lived alone, spending all her time scrubbing and sweeping her little house until it shone.

One night as she was sweeping, there came a knock at her door. She opened it to find three strangely dressed men. From their crowns and robes, she guessed they might be Kings. They explained to her that they were on their way to Bethlehem, following a brilliant star, to worship a newborn King. The Kings invited her to join them on the journey. "I am much too busy to go away on a holiday," she said, "for I have not yet finished my sweeping." But the next day, she promised, she would surely start off and meet up with them.

The next morning, having finished her work, the Befana thought of her trip. She remembered seeing gifts the Kings were carrying, and she felt she, too, would like to bring a gift to the baby. Her greatest treasure was a chest of toys that had belonged to her own child. She opened this chest and looked sadly at each of the toys. Though she was not really sure she could bear to part with them, she finally chose a tattered little doll and a ball.

She packed the toys into a basket, along with herbs for the child's mother, and set off on her journey. She searched and searched, but no matter how hard she looked, she could find neither the Three Kings nor the baby. On and on she wandered, until she had quite thoroughly lost her way. And still she did not stop. Wearing her kerchief and carrying her basket and her broom, she searches even now, on every Epiphany Eve.

The Befana visits the home of every Italian child to see if he might be the one she is looking for. Although she is always disappointed, she leaves a little gift anyway, in memory of the Christ Child.

Fairs and markets in Italy sell special Befana dolls, which are little old women carrying baskets and brooms. In many piazzas, or squares, such as the Piazza Navona in Rome, there is a Christmas fair, with a real Befana, who gives gifts of candy or charcoal to the children who come to her little house, just as children in the United States visit Santa Claus.

(116)

BEFANA DOLL

Materials: Two colors of crepe paper or fabric, darning needle, carpet thread, cellophane tape, colored pencils or felt pens, construction paper, rubber cement, straight pins, scissors, stiff cardboard, twig or piece of straw, colored or white pipe cleaners, pencil, ruler, cardboard tube (wax paper, etc.). *Note:* Befana doll may be as large as you like; use any length tube, adjust measurements to fit.

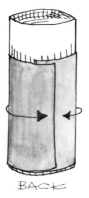

1. Draw Befana's face and hair on tube as shown, with colored pencils or felt pens.

2. Measure distance from bottom of chin to bottom of tube. Cut a piece of colored paper this width and long enough to wrap around tube, overlapping ends in back. Be sure seam is in back. Spread glue on tube and overlapped ends and press to hold in place. Cover tube completely from chin down.

BACK

3. Twist two pipe cleaners together as shown (a). A short distance below chin, mark armholes on opposite sides of tube. With scissors point or sharp pencil, poke holes in marks (b). Push twisted pipe cleaner through holes, pull out equal length on each side for arms (c). To secure arms in place, make "shoulders" by twisting pipe cleaner, where it comes out of tube, once around into a loop; press loops flat against tube. Then bend arms out at angle to body. Twist hand loops at pipe cleaner ends (d).

(117)

4. To make base, cut stiff cardboard square or circle about 1″ larger around than tube. Put aside until last step.

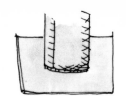

5. Prepare tube for base by covering tube bottom: Stand tube on construction paper. Measure tube width (a), then cut a strip of paper this wide and long enough to wrap up at least 2″ on each side of tube. Taper sides of strip as shown. Spread glue on tube sides and on tapered strip ends (b). Fold tapered ends up, pressing firmly to tube as shown, covering bottom neatly (c).

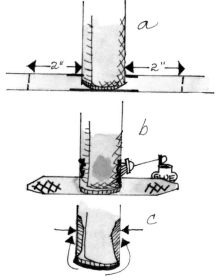

6. For skirt length, measure crepe paper (grain running vertically) or fabric from just under arms to bottom of tube. Add 1″ for hem. To measure width, wrap paper around tube at least four or five times (skirt must be wide enough to gather), then cut. To gather skirt, fold over 1″ at top long edge; thread needle with carpet thread, knot one end (see page 19), and take big gathering stitches as shown (a) across hem. When you reach the end, remove needle. Hold thread, and push paper along it to gather (b). Wrap gathered skirt, hem up, around tube just under arms. Wind loose thread end around waist to hold; tie thread to itself or tape. Spread out fullness of skirt (c).

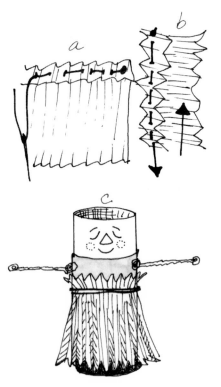

(118)

7. For apron, cut contrasting color crepe paper or fabric in shape indicated (length shorter than skirt). Be sure to make ties long enough to tie around waist.

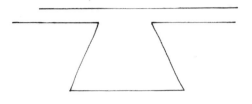

8. Place apron in front (a), wrap ties around waist covering thread, and tie in knot in back (b). Trim ends if they are too long.

9. For kerchief, cut strip of crepe paper (grain horizontal) or fabric 3½″ wide, at least 12″ long. Center strip on head and fold it over forehead (a). Smooth fold over forehead, tuck corners in toward tube, then pull ends of strip forward and tie as shown (b). To hold knot in place, glue, or push straight pin through knot into tube.

10. Spread glue on covered tube bottom and on center of cardboard base (step 4). Press glued surfaces together, standing doll up firmly upon base.

11. To make broom, split ends of twig or straw (a), or cut out a paper broom (b). Twist pipe cleaner arm around to hold broom.

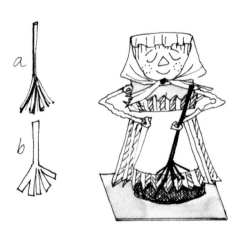

(119)

Another Epiphany tradition is the "bean cake," in which a charm, or bean, is hidden. Good luck and special favors go to the one who finds the bean in his portion of cake. The bean cake had its origin in the ancient Roman festival of Saturnalia (see page 60), at which a large plum cake was served. Whoever found the bean hidden in his piece of plum cake was called "The King of the Bean," and ruled over the festivities for the next twelve days.

In France, children look forward to celebrating *Épiphanie* with the customary *Galette des Rois* (gah-let day rwah), or "Kings' Cake." Inside this puff pastry cake a *fève* (fehv), or bean, is baked. Originally, a tiny porcelain figurine of Jesus was used, and for this reason, the fève is sometimes called a *Jésus* (Jay-sú). Whoever finds the fève in his portion of cake is given a golden paper crown, and becomes the *Roi de la Fève* (rwah de lah fehv), "King of the Bean," or *Reine* (ren), "Queen." If a girl finds the fève, she must choose a King, or the King must choose a Queen, and the royal couple exchange little gifts.

GALETTE DES ROIS *(Epiphany Bean Cake)*

Materials: Prepared cake or brownie mix, frosting (see page 133), whole dried large bean (lima or kidney) or whole blanched almond, baking pans—round or circular tube pan (crown shaped).

In France, the Galette des Rois is made from a special puff pastry. A similar effect may be had more easily by using any prepared cake or brownie mix. Follow directions on the package; after batter is prepared, pour it into baking pan. Then drop one large dried bean or whole shelled almond into one layer. Stir batter around and bake as directed. Decorate cake with design of crown on top. Serve cake at party, and give crown (opposite) and/or small gift to whomever finds nut or bean in his portion.

COURONNE *(Epiphany Crown)*

Materials: Gold colored stiff paper, scissors, pencil, stapler.

1. Cut strip of gold paper 3″ by 24″.

2. Trace pattern and transfer (see page 18) design three times to strip. Each time you move tracing design along strip, carefully join both halves of point X.

3. Cut design out, simplifying shapes if necessary, to suit abilities of crown-maker.

4. Pull strip around into circle, gold color outside. Overlap ends to fit head and staple. Glue on paper "jewels" if desired.

In England, Epiphany, the twelfth day after Christmas, is usually known as Twelfth Night, and a "beanfeast" is a popular custom. In many places, parties or banquets are held, and the traditional bean cake served. Whoever finds the bean in his portion becomes the King or Queen, as in France, and must choose a mate. The royal couple then choose a court: ministers, ladies or lords-in-waiting, and a court fool to amuse everyone during the party.

The last of Twelve Days of Christmas, Twelfth Night, marks the end of the Christmas festivities. This is the day in many countries when decorations are removed, for it is believed to be bad luck to leave them up a day longer. Although in the United States, gifts are usually exchanged on Christmas Day, the Twelfth Day of Christmas is a special day and one on which it might be fun to receive a special gift. One might begin a new Twelfth Night tradition by making a "Twelve Days of Christmas" mobile, following the directions below. Gifts hanging on the mobile may be shared on this day at a "beanfeast" party. A bean cake may be served, and larger gifts given to the King and Queen along with a paper crown.

TWELVE DAYS OF CHRISTMAS MOBILE

Materials: Five wooden dowels or sticks: three—6" long, one—16" long, one—24" long, white bristol board, exacto knife, cellophane tape, scissors, colored felt pens or crayons or tempera paints and brush, small lightweight gifts (to fit in boxes), newspaper, darning needle, carpet thread.

1. Trace pattern on page 125. Transfer (see page 18) 12 times to bristol board. Cut out along solid lines.

2. Score *dotted lines* (see page 19).

3. Place cut boxes flat, *scored lines up*, on newspaper. Decorate, using suggested patterns on facing page, or making up your own designs—one box for each day of "Twelve Days of Christmas" song.

(122)

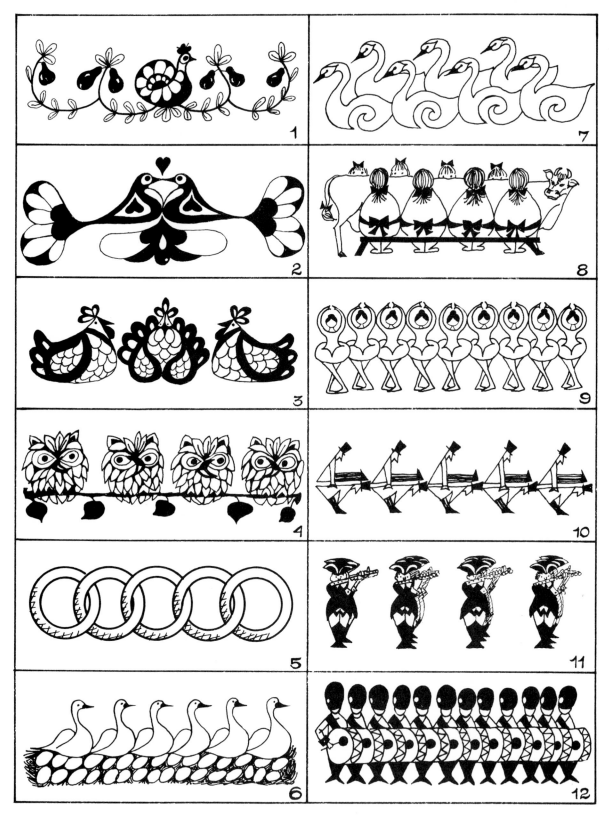

4. When designs are complete, fold up box and glue flap marked X to inside. Leave one end of box open.

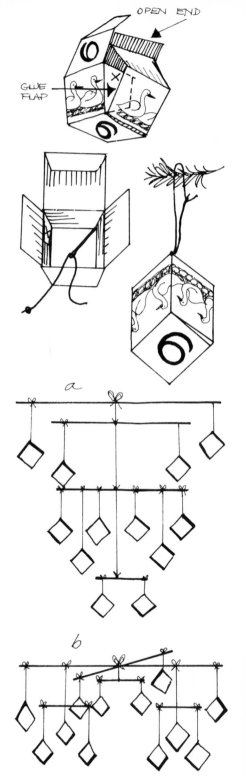

5. Before filling or closing box, knot (see page 19) one end of long carpet thread and stitch once through inside corner of box as shown (or through top). Keeping knot inside box, remove needle. End of thread will later be tied onto mobile or Christmas tree.

6. Fill each box with small gift. Close box and tape with cellophane tape if necessary.

7. To make mobile: Find center of longest (24″) stick. Tie carpet thread around it, leaving one long end for hanging mobile up. Tie long threads (lengths depend upon size of mobile) from center of each remaining stick; hang this stick from hook or tape to ceiling while adding other sticks and boxes. Tie on other sticks and boxes as shown, (a) and (b), or improvise your own design. Remember, *mobile must balance*. Slide threads along sticks, and slide boxes also, until entire mobile is in balance.

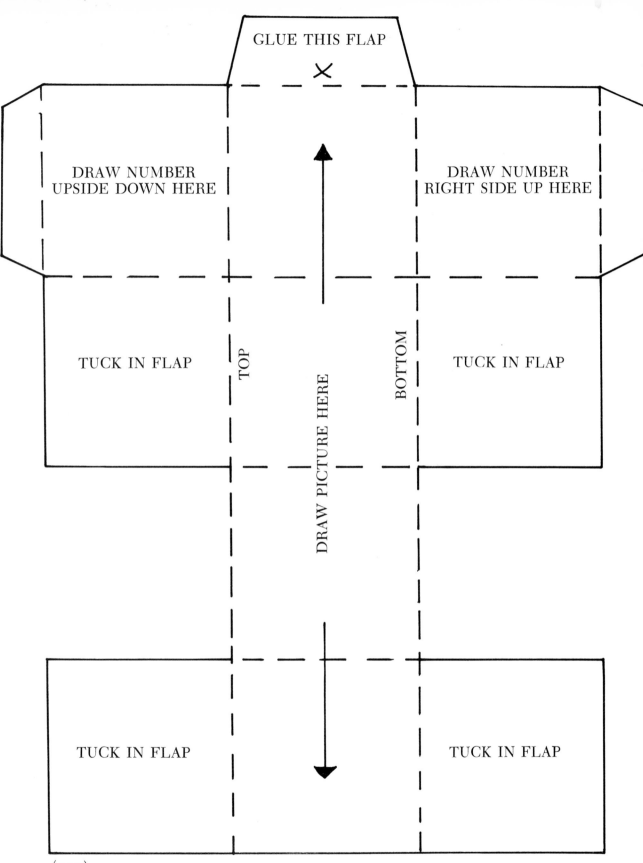

Valentine's Day

February, which breaks into winter with the very first signs of spring, has long been a time for celebrations. In ancient Rome, the fifteenth of the month was the day of the Lupercalia festival. On this date, priests, known as Luperci, performed a special ceremony for the sheepherding community living atop the Palatine Hill. At the cave of the Lupercal, sacrifices were made of goats and a dog, after which two young Luperci ran about the base of the hill with strips of the animal hides, called "februa" (origin of word "February"), touching all they met. They thus imparted fertility to the women, and traced a kind of magic circle about the hill to keep evil spirits, and especially wild wolves, away.

Other special festivities were also held on this day, as it was the beginning of spring and long believed to be the day on which birds chose their mates. This fact, combined with the magical fertility rites of Lupercalia, combined to make February 15 a special holiday for lovers. Roman boys and girls put their names in an urn, drew the slips, and selected their sweethearts for the next year. When the Roman Empire spread to England, the custom of drawing lots continued, with the addition that there, when a boy drew a girl's name, he pinned it to his sleeve, giving us the expression "wearing your heart on your sleeve." Often, the "pinned" sweethearts eventually married.

The exact identity of the man for whom St. Valentine's Day is named is not known. We do know that there were two Christians named Valentine, one a priest, one a bishop, both of whom were martyred by Emperor Claudius II in Rome in the third century A.D., on the fourteenth of February. Both men are buried in Rome. Several legends are offered from which to choose an explanation for the holiday's name. One story tells that Roman soldiers refused to go off to fight in Emperor Claudius's wars because they did not want to leave their wives and sweethearts. The cruel Emperor then forbade marriages and canceled all engagements; but a bishop named Valentine helped the lovers by secretly continuing to perform marriages. When he was discovered, Claudius had him thrown in prison, where he died. Another story tells that Valentine was a priest, jailed for helping Christians. While in jail, he cured his jailer's daughter of blindness. Some say he also fell in love with the girl, and wrote her love notes. In any case, before he died, he wrote a final note to her, signed "from your Valentine." Claudius was furious when he heard of the girl's cure by a Christian, and had Valentine beheaded on February 14, A.D. 269. Others say Valentine died February 14, A.D. 270, for refusing to give up Christianity. In A.D. 496 Pope Gelasius set February 14 as the date on which to honor the good Saint Valentine. Because of the nearness of the dates, many customs of the pagan lovers' holiday, Lupercalia, were carried into the celebration of St. Valentine's Day. The custom of sending cards, or "valentines," however, comes from the note which Valentine wrote to the jailer's daughter, and when you sign your cards "from your valentine," you are carrying on an old tradition.

One of the most enchanting old-fashioned valentines is the *tussie mussie*, a nosegay of sweet-smelling and symbolic herbs. The tussie mussie first appeared in England in the 1600's, and remained popular there, and later in the United States, until the end of the nineteenth century. Originally, a single flower was placed in the center of the bouquet, surrounded by a variety of buds and herbs, each with its special meaning. A very specific message could be sent, from loving to spiteful, depending on which plants were selected. The custom was especially popular during the Victorian period in the 1800's, when many books were published explaining the symbolic meanings of flowers and herbs. These meanings go back to such ancient cultures as Greece, Rome, China, and India, where plant symbolism was important in medicine and witchcraft as well as popular folklore. The meanings of the herbs and flowers often vary, depending upon which country or source one consults. Some, of course, are constant, and in any case, the preferred meaning may be chosen and included in a little explanation sent with the tussie mussie to your modern valentine, who might otherwise miss the subtleties of your message.

TUSSIE MUSSIE

As it is highly unlikely that one will have on hand in February all the fresh herbs and flowers necessary to make a live tussie mussie, the only practical solution is to draw them. On the front of your card, copy following sketches, choosing appropriate plants for your valentine message bouquet. On the inside of your card, you might perhaps include a short glossary of the plants and their meanings.

Materials: Colored paper, scissors, crayons or colored felt pens, and a ready-made envelope (large enough to contain your card).

1. Cut colored or white paper at least 10″ by 6½″. Bring short ends together, folding in half to 5″ by 6½″.

2. On front of card, copy selected plants in a traditional nosegay as shown, or in any arrangement you like.

3. Inside card, explain plant meanings as shown.

DAFFODIL—Regard

ROSE—Love

PANSY—Think of Me

RUE—Understanding

SAGE—Long Life

IVY—Marriage, Friendship

SWEET MARJORAM—
Blushes, Joy

CHRYSANTHEMUM *(red)*—
I Love You

BASIL—Love, Hate

ROSEMARY—Remembrance

THYME—Courage

VIOLET—Faithfulness

In the United States, handmade valentines and verses began to appear around 1740. They were of all designs and shapes, sealed with red wax, and either left secretly upon one's lover's doorstep or sent by stagecoach mail. Some of the most unusual early valentines were made by the Pennsylvania-Germans. These creative people specialized in cutout and pinprick designs, made into elaborate valentine cards, marriage and birth certificates, and religious and decorative panels. Some designs were bold and simple, with a heart motif, a few pinprick whirls, and a single bright color. Others were more complex, with birds, hearts, tulips, and angels, painted many brilliant shades of watercolor. The Pennsylvania-German valentines were made up until the 1850's, when throughout the United States, commercially-made cards appeared, using lithography and wood-cutting techniques. From this time on, store-bought valentines began to replace the handmade, until now, the handmade card is a truly rare and precious token of love.

PENNSYLVANIA-GERMAN VALENTINES

Materials: Red construction paper, scissors, thin, easily folded colored or white paper (typing paper, for example), darning needle, rubber cement, watercolors and brush, old magazine, pinking shears or manicure scissors, exacto knife.

DESIGN I

1. Cut piece of thin paper (not construction paper) 8½″ square (see page 20, Method I).

2. Fold paper in half (a), then in half again (b). Holding paper in this position, fold paper along diagonal as shown (c).

3. Keeping folded paper in same position, draw gently curved line across tops as shown (a). Cut along line (b).

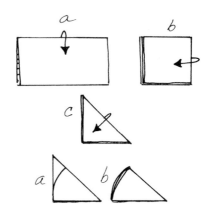

4. Place paper *point down, keeping single fold edge on right.* Trace pattern A (outline *and* patterned areas) from page 132. Tape tracing over folded paper, lining up shapes in identical positions to pattern, and transfer design (see page 18).

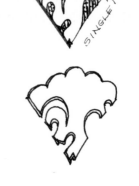

5. Cut around outlines of all transferred patterned areas.

6. Unfold paper gently and smooth flat an old magazine. With pencil, very lightly sketch a design to be pinpricked around cutouts, as shown.

7. Keeping paper over magazine, with darning needle, prick holes along sketched lines as shown.

8. If desired, decorate designs with watercolors, or leave plain. When dry, mount on red construction paper.

DESIGN II

1. Fold 8½″ square (see page 20, Method I) paper in half and tape edges down on table. Trace pattern B from page 132.

2. Line "fold" edge (dotted line) of tracing up with folded paper edge; tape tracing over folded paper and transfer design (see page 18).

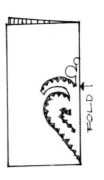

3. To cut out design, use pinking shears to cut jagged edges *or* cut plain basic outline and then cut tiny wedges out around edge with manicure scissors.

4. Unfold cut paper and spread flat on old magazine. Complete as in Design I, steps 6, 7, and 8.

DESIGN III

1. Follow Design I, steps 1, 2, and 3.

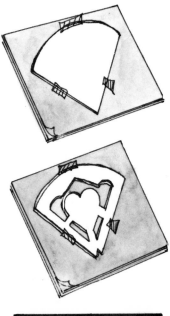

2. Keeping single fold of wedge on *right*, tape paper onto magazine. *Note:* Place tape lightly on edges of paper.

3. Trace pattern C, page 132. Line up edges of tracing with folded paper and transfer design (see page 18).

4. Remove tracing, but leave folded paper taped to magazine. With exacto knife (which is dangerous and should not be used without permission or adult supervision), cut out transferred design removing all dotted areas of pattern.

5. Remove tape and spread design flat on magazine. Complete as in Design I, steps 6, 7, and 8.

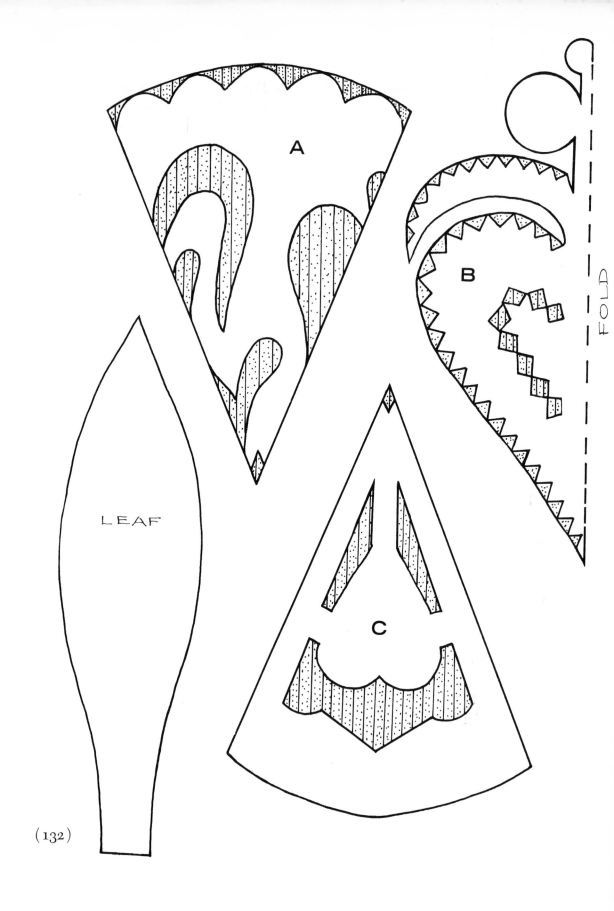

A

B

C

LEAF

FOLD

(132)

In Hungary, while there is no Valentine's Day as we know it, a special love token, called *mézeskalács* (maiz'-esh-koh-latch'), is sold throughout the year. This special honey cake, which looks somewhat like a large decorated gingerbread cookie, is sold mainly at country fairs. A sort of valentine, the mézeskalács is always given as a token of affection. It is made in two traditional shapes: the heart—primarily bought by boys for their girl friends; and the hussar, or cavalry captain—bought by parents for their young boys. The cookie is decorated with sugar icing, the base color usually being the brilliant red traditional in Hungarian folk art, with flowers and trimming in red, white, yellow, and blue. Tiny mirrors are "glued" on with icing, as are bits of paper (the hussar's face, angels, etc.) for added decoration. Often the traditional *szivküldi szivnek* (seev-kul'-dee seev-nek'), "heart sends it to heart," is written with icing upon the heart.

MÉZESKALÁCS *(Hungarian Cookie)*

DECORATIVE FROSTING

Ingredients: 2 cups sifted confectioners' sugar
1 egg white
juice of ¼ lemon
vegetable food coloring

Equipment: Mixing bowl, electric beater or wire whisk, spoon, measuring cup, several small bowls or cups, small mirror (to decorate heart).

1. Separate egg and place white in mixing bowl. Refrigerate yolk for later use.

2. Beat egg white fluffy with wire whisk or electric beater.

3. Slowly add sugar, then lemon juice, beating with spoon when frosting begins to get stiff.

(133)

4. Add food coloring, or spoon frosting into several small bowls or cups and add a few drops of different color into each.

5. Spoon colored frosting into cloth or paper decorator's frosting tube (see below), and roll end over. Squeeze rolled bag until sufficient frosting has come out to make decoration, then lift bag up and release pressure to stop flow of frosting.

6. To make cookie, use any gingerbread dough, cupcake, or regular sugar cookie dough (see page 82).

7. Before decorating final mézeskalács, experiment with several flowers and border designs on wax paper. After deciding upon final design, squeeze decorations directly onto cookie. Set aside until frosting has hardened.

8. To attach small mirror, spread small amount of frosting on backside of mirror and on cookie in spot where it will be placed. Press "glued" surfaces together and allow frosting to harden.

DECORATOR'S FROSTING TUBE

Materials: Wax paper, scotch or masking tape, scissors.

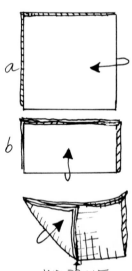

1. Cut piece of wax paper 12″ by 20″. Fold in half, bringing short ends together (a). Fold in half once again, as shown (b).

2. Place paper flat on table with long folded edge toward you, as shown. Turn bottom left corner up and over toward center.

3. Keeping mid-point tightly rolled, proceed to roll left flap over to right as shown (a) and (b).

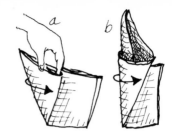

4. Tape end of paper over onto side of cone.

5. Cut tiny notch or leave round shape in end of cone for decorating tip. If it is too small to allow frosting through easily, cut tip slightly larger.

6. After spooning frosting into tube, fold down flap (a), roll down to compact frosting, and push on roll with thumbs to force out frosting (b).

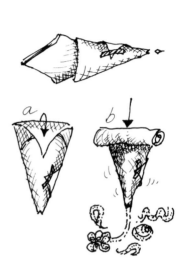

In Wales, we find another unique love token given by sweethearts throughout the year. The Welsh "Love Spoon" is a specially carved wooden spoon hanging from a carved panel or handle, given by young men to their girl friends as a sign of courtship. An attractive girl might have a whole collection of decorative spoons from admirers. The tradition originated in the seventeenth century, and became especially popular in the eighteenth and nineteenth centuries. Many of the fine early examples may be seen in the National Museum of Wales. Although the custom is fading now in some parts of the country, the occasional specialist in spoon carving may still be found. Nesting spoons of graduated sizes fitting closely together provided the inspiration for the spoon to become a symbol of love, and gave the English language the expression "to spoon," meaning "to court."

Welsh love spoons are carved from many different kinds of local woods, from sycamore to evergreen, and the motifs used in the panels are traditional. A "wheel of fortune" with a heart in the center indicates the sender's willingness to work and share all his wealth. Two spoon bowls coming down from one handle, or one bowl shaped like a heart with a rib in the middle, means "we two are one." A small house or keyhole design means "my house is yours." The bowl carved into a spade shape means "I will dig for you." Several bowls coming off a large handle signify a desire for a large family. If the carver is a sailor, the spoon may have an anchor, or ship, carved among the hearts and comma-shaped "soul symbols." The soul symbols are an ancient Egyptian symbol representing the nostrils, through which the soul was believed to escape at death. (It is not known how this symbol came to be used in Wales.) The love spoon was never meant to be a useful object, nor was it meant to replace the engagement ring. It was, and is, a token of intent, an imaginatively created "wooden love letter."

WHEEL   TWO ARE ONE   KEYHOLE   SPADE   SOUL SYMBOLS

WELSH LOVE SPOONS

While these love tokens are traditionally carved from wood, a similar effect may be obtained more easily by modeling in self-hardening clay. A wood texture or any other color finish may be painted on and shellacked.

Materials: Self-hardening clay, tempera paint, brush, shellac and brush, alcohol (solvent for shellac), old rolling pin or round bottle (optional), old table knife or blockprinting tool, ruler, pencil.

1. Read and follow directions on package of self-hardening clay.

2. Before modeling clay, make sketches on scrap paper to determine size and shape of spoon, handle, and motifs for design. To model clay, begin with large lump and roll or pat it into a long rectangle (in our example, ½" thick, 4" wide by 8½" long).

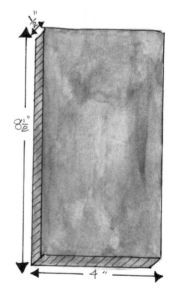

3. With point of pencil, sketch design into surface of clay. Keep shapes bold. Dot surface of areas to be cut away. *Note:* Sketch outline design of handle as well as inside design and spoons.

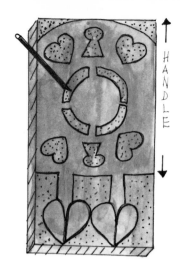

4. With knife or block printing tool, cut out and/or scratch design into handle. *Note:* If you are cutting away certain sections completely, be sure to leave large enough solid areas *between* holes to keep handle strong.

5. Cut around outline of handle, and around spoons as shown.

6. Model spoon bowls by pressing inside round with finger. Trim spoon edges with knife if spoons get too big when shaping. *Note:* Do not make spoon bowls too thin or they will crack when dry. For extra strength, if using more than one spoon bowl, attach sides of spoons to each other (arrow) with slip (a creamy mixture of clay and water).

7. Smooth out any rough edges, add finishing touches such as border lines around cut shapes, traced with pencil. Etch with pencil the name of your valentine, date, or "I love you." Set spoon aside to dry. Complete, paint and shellac, following steps 4 and 5, page 47.

(137)

Mardi Gras
Carnival

Carnival time includes the entire period between Epiphany (January 6) and Shrove Tuesday. These weeks just before Lent have special importance as a last chance for feasting and fun, for the forty days which immediately precede Easter are known as Lent, a solemn time of self-denial for Christians. This is a time for prayer and fasting, when pleasures are denied. The carnival, or "Mardi Gras" season is famous throughout the Christian world for processions, feasting, and gay masquerades—all activities indulged in by the early pagans during their spring holidays to insure healthy crops.

Both words "carnival" and "Mardi Gras" are derived from the Christian meaning of the holiday. "Carnival" comes from the Latin *carnelevamen*, meaning "taking away of the meat," and refers to the time when Lent was observed by strict fasts. Gradually, the word came to mean the days just before Lent. *Mardi Gras*, from the French, literally means "fat Tuesday." It is so named because all butter and fats had to be used up by Shrove Tuesday, the day before the start of Lent.

Mardi Gras celebrations around the world are endlessly varied and intriguing. One of the most unusual is the Shrove Tuesday Pancake Race in Olney, Buckinghamshire, England. Pancake-making became a Shrove Tuesday tradition in England in order to use up the dairy products forbidden during Lent. Legend tells that the Olney pancake race had its origin in the year 1445, when a local woman was so late for church, she forgot to put down her frying pan and ran all the way to the church carrying her pancake. Today, races are run in other English towns as well, and in the United States, the women of Liberal, Kansas, race in direct competition with the women of Olney, England, comparing their results.

In Olney, the main event is started by the official costumed Ringer of the Pancake Bell. Competitors wear the traditional costume of apron and kerchief, and must toss their pancake three times while running the 415-yard course from the parish pump to the church porch, a feat usually accomplished in about one minute. A second bell sounds the end of the race, and the winner receives a kiss from the Bell Ringer.

PANCAKE RACE COSTUMES

Bell Ringer (One boy): Red shirt, jacket or coat, preferably with brass or yellow buttons, or with brass-colored paper circles pinned over buttons down front; small pillow stuffed inside jacket front for big belly; row of various colored medals pinned on chest (see page 37); hat—any decorative helmet or cap; bell.

Judges (the other boys in group): One extra-large paper medal (labeled "judge") worn on chest (see page 37).

Girl Racers: Full skirt, blouse, apron tied around waist, kerchief tied around head.

PANCAKES

Materials: Small (8″ or less) lightweight frying pans, scissors, stiff cardboard, crayons, paints or colored paper, and glue.

Cut a cardboard circle to fit the bottom of each pan. It should fit loosely enough to move easily when pan is shaken. Paint or color each side of "pancake" a different color, so judges can see it flip over.

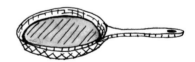

RACE

Girl racers line up behind starting line, each holding her frying pan containing a pancake. Bell Ringer stands to one side of starting line, holding bell. Judges are scattered along race path and at finish line to observe. Start is signaled by Bell Ringer's bell. Racers run along path holding frying pans out in front of them and must, during the course, flip their pancakes three (3) times. If pancake falls, or if it is not flipped, judges disqualify racer. Whoever reaches finish line first following all rules, receives the prize.

New Orleans has one of the most famous carnival celebrations in the United States. The holiday begins on Twelfth Night, January 6, and lasts four weeks, until Mardi Gras—the last and biggest day of the festivities. Fantastic parades are held; everyone participates, and school children as well as adults build floats and elect a King and Queen to preside over the various activities. Men's societies, called "krewes," organize elaborate costume balls, build floats, and parade in costume. Each year, the parade chooses a different theme, such as "Fairy Tales," to unify the design of the floats. Mardi Gras is a legal holiday in Alabama, Louisiana, and Florida.

In other countries, costume parades are also popular. In France, Spain, and Italy, flowers are used to decorate floats and costumes, and "wars" of flower-throwing are held. In some Austrian villages, costumed children parade on skis, for there is still snow at carnival time. In certain German towns, costumed "witches" parade carrying brooms with which they sweep the streets, symbolizing the ancient tradition of chasing evil spirits by spring cleaning. The most famous carnival in Switzerland is held in the city of Basle. Elaborate costume parades exhibit some of the most original masks ever created. One of the most unusual, for example, is the double mask, really a face mask with a sort of second masked head mounted on top. Often these upper masks are made to satirize local politicians or local events; one marching group will choose a particular organization it wishes to poke fun at, and each marcher will make his mask resemble a member of that group.

BASLE DOUBLE MASK

Materials: 11"-long cardboard tube, colored construction paper, colored wool, masking tape, and complete list of materials from Paper-Bag Masks, page 24.

1. To make the first mask, follow steps 1–8 of *Paper-Bag Mask* directions, page 24, (not King or Queen Variations), *except* in step 5. Do *not* cut out the feather, but leave hat top *whole.*

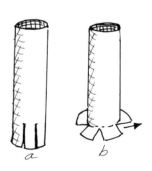

2. To make holder for second set of masks: In the bottom edge of cardboard tube, make five evenly spaced cuts about 1" long as shown (a). Bend fringe up and out (b).

3. Cut hole in center of top of hat, just big enough for tube (a). Push tube up through inside of hat as shown (b), until fringe catches on inside of top. Tape across tube fringe, anchoring it firmly to inside hat top.

4. Turn hat right-side up. On bottom of tube, mark off "neck" space about 1½" high.

5. To make second set of masks: Sketch shape of mask on colored paper (it should be about 10" high and at least 5" wide). Using folded paper or two layers held together, cut two of these shapes exactly the same size, as shown. Shapes will be stapled together around central tube.

6. With crayons, felt pens, etc., decorate both cutout shapes. You can have a 2-faced mask (one in front, one in back) or a face on one side, back of head on other.

7. Brush a line of rubber cement over front and back of tube *from neck line up to top.* Brush rubber cement along center line of *underside* of each mask.

8. Decide which mask goes on front of tube. Place this, *face down,* on table. Lining up chin with tube's "neck" line, press glued *front* of tube down onto *glued back* of face. Press *glued back* of second face onto *glued back* of tube.

9. Staple together both pairs of ears. Staple top of heads together and cover with glued-on wool "hair" if desired.

10. Draw collar on tube's "neck," or cut out, decorate, and glue on a paper bow tie. Wear mask as described in *Paper-Bag Mask* directions, page 25, steps 7 and 8.

(141)

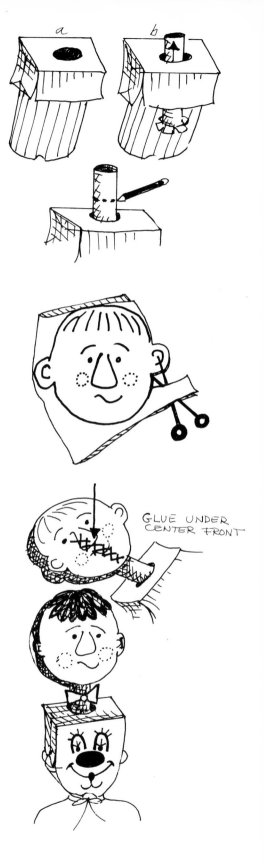

GLUE UNDER CENTER FRONT

 # SPRING

The arrival of spring, signaled by the vernal equinox, when the sun crosses the celestial equator, has always been a time for celebration. The Druids, a Celtic nature-worshiping people who lived in what is now the British Isles, divided their year by two main feasts: Samhain, the feast of late autumn (see *Halloween*, page 23), and Beltane, the festival of spring, dedicated to the god Belenos, whose symbol was fire. The Beltane ritual included the lighting of bonfires, called "beltane fires," whose magic power and light protected against witchcraft and encouraged the sun to return warmth to the earth. A modern Society of Druids in England still observes these seasonal changes at the sites used by their ancestors in ancient times. At Stonehenge, for example, bonfires are held at the beginning of May to welcome spring and the start of new life. Many Eastern nations celebrate their new year at this time. In fact, it was as recently as 1752 that Great Britain and her American Colonies accepted January 1 instead of the traditional March 25, as the New Year. (See *April 1,* page 149).

Ancient Greek and Roman mythology also tell of battles between the forces of winter and spring. Today, many countries have special ceremonies reflecting these battles and the Druid rites on the night of the spring equinox. The bad forces of the long cold winter must be driven away and the sun, with its warm spring, encouraged to stay.

After spring has in fact arrived, festivals have traditionally been held to honor the fruits and flowers brought with it. The first days of April and May have long been dedicated to this purpose. And Easter, long before it became a Christian holiday honoring the rebirth of Christ, was a pagan celebration of nature's rebirth after winter.

Sechseläeuten

In Zurich, Switzerland, the arrival of spring is celebrated on the third Monday in April with the festival of Sechseläeuten (sek'-se-loy-tin). The name means "Six o'clock bells," and refers to the bells of the Great Cathedral of Zurich which were rung years ago (on the first Monday following the spring equinox) to announce the beginning of the spring festival. Today, the celebration lasts two days. On Sunday, the people of the city gather to watch the children's parade; boys and girls over five years old parade in all types of costumes, as we do on Halloween. On Monday afternoon, a parade of guildsmen (representing all the professions) in their historical costumes, and gaily bedecked children march to the main square. Here the climax of the celebration takes place: a white cotton effigy, or dummy, of a snowman is waiting, wearing his top hat, smoking a pipe, and carrying a broom. Called *Böögg* (beuk), or "Old Man Winter," he is stuffed inside with firecrackers, and sits upon a bonfire which is lit as soon as the *sechseläeuten* begin to ring. As Böögg burns, costumed boys on horseback gallop madly around the fire. Old Man Winter has been destroyed, and the merrymaking and feasting to welcome spring go on late into the night.

BÖÖGG *(Old Man Winter)*

For a Welcome to Spring party, or a February or March birthday, cotton or ice cream snowmen may be made as favors for each guest, or one large cotton snowman may be made for a centerpiece. To symbolize winter's end, the ice cream snowmen may be eaten, or those of cotton thrown away or, *with careful adult supervision*, burned in a fireplace.

ICE CREAM SNOWMEN

1. Stack three scooped balls of vanilla ice cream into a snowman. Make one for each guest.

2. Decorate face and buttons with chocolate candies.

3. Set snowmen on plate or tray and place in freezer until party. Before serving, a whole marshmallow, tinted with food coloring, may be stuck into head with a toothpick, making snowman's hat.

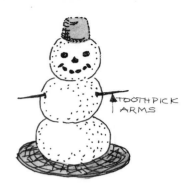

TOOTHPICK ARMS

COTTON SNOWMAN

Materials: Absorbent cotton (balls or roll), colored and black construction paper, scissors, Elmer's or Sobo glue (*do not use rubber cement if you plan to burn cotton snowman, its fumes are harmful to breathe*), tempera paint, brush.

1. To make base, cut piece of colored construction paper in roughly 3″ square (see page 20, Method I).

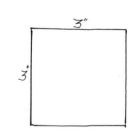

2. Pull small wads of cotton off roll and form into three balls, each about 2″ across. To make a smooth ball, pull cotton fibers over top of ball, gather ends together at bottom and hold with dabs of Elmer's or Sobo glue.

3. Spread several drops of glue in center of paper base and press on one cotton ball, glued ends down.

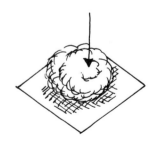

4. Spread a few drops of glue in a ring on top of this ball as shown (a) and press another cotton ball on top of glue (b).

5. Repeat steps 4 (a) and (b) to add the last cotton ball.

6. Using very *little* water, so paint is thick, paint face and buttons on snowman as shown. *Note:* When applying paint to cotton, carefully dab with point of brush; if you sweep bristles across, fine cotton fibers will lift up and smear design.

7. To make hat cut a 1½″ square of black paper. Also cut a strip of black paper about 3″ long and 1″ wide.

8. Fold long strip up about ½″ on each end as shown, curving the middle up.

9. Spread glue on *underside* of each folded end. Press glued ends down onto flat square, curving central part of strip up as shown.

10. Spread several drops of glue over the top of snowman's head and press hat on head, as shown.

Swedish Spring

In Sweden, where the winter is long and hard, spring is eagerly awaited. Although snow is on the ground when Lent begins, its arrival is a sign that spring cannot be too far behind. To urge spring to hurry, the Swedes have a lovely custom, of ancient origin, called *Påsk Ris* (poohsk rees), or "Easter Twigs." Birch or beech branches are cut, brought inside, and set in water. Then brightly colored chicken or rooster feathers are tied all over the twigs. The gaily feathered branches may also be bought in the marketplaces. The warmth of the house soon forces buds to appear, and by Easter, the leaves which have sprouted amid the feathers are regarded as the first real sign of spring. Its official arrival, however, is celebrated on Walpurgis Night, April 30. Adults and children rejoice with singing, dancing, and the lighting of bonfires just as their Viking ancestors did centuries before. Light from the mountaintop bonfires welcomes the sun and chases away the spirits of darkness and winter.

PÅSK RIS *(Easter Twigs)*

Material: Branches of forsythia, birch, beech, pussywillow, or whatever other non-evergreen branches you can find in the woods or at the florist's in February, at the start of Lenten season; colored feathers of any sort, thin wire or carpet thread, scissors, large vase full of water, hammer.

1. Spread woody branches on newspaper, hammer the ends to split them so they may readily absorb water.

2. Cut several short lengths of wire or thread and tie one end of each strand around the end of a feather. Tie colored feathers onto branches.

3. Stand feathered branches in vase of water at the beginning of Lent, and by Easter leaves will have begun to sprout.

(146)

Hina-Matsuri

In Japan, spring is a time of special children's festivals. The Peach Festival, or *Hina-Matsuri* (hee-nah-mah-tsu-ree) on March 3, is also the day of the "Girls' Doll Festival." On this day doll collections are brought out and elaborately displayed. They often incude an emperor, his empress, and their attendants. Many dolls have porcelain heads and are family treasures, handed down from mother to daughter. Young girls visit one another on this day to admire their dolls, have doll tea parties, and compliment each other on their peach blossom decorations. The peach symbolizes happiness in marriage, representing the qualities of mildness and peacefulness all girls hope to acquire.

EGGSHELL PUPPET

The eggshell which forms this puppet's head has a whiteness and delicacy which resembles that of the porcelain-headed Japanese dolls.

Materials: White egg, fine sewing needle, bowl, small pointed manicure scissors, cotton cloth, rubber cement, masking tape, fine pointed felt pens or tempera paint and small brush, thin colored wool, pencil.

1. With needle, gently poke small hole, about ¼″ across, in top and bottom of egg, as shown, and blow contents into bowl.

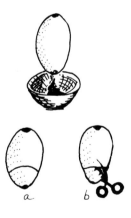

2. Wash and dry egg. With felt pen or pencil, draw line around egg about one third up from bottom of egg (narrow end) (a). Stick point of manicure scissors into *bottom* hole and slowly and carefully cut up from the bottom and around the drawn line (b).

3. If inside of remaining shell is wet, dry gently with tissue. Then with finger, spread rubber cement all over inside of shell; this coating will help keep egg from cracking.

4. Cut a circle of fabric about 16″ across (see page 20, Method I or II). Fold circle in half, then in half once more (a). Cut off about ½″ of tip X (b).

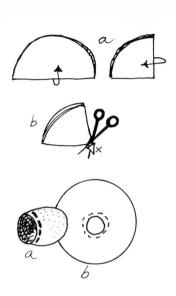

5. Open circle and, if necessary, enlarge hole in center until *just* large enough to fit around open end of eggshell.

6. Spread rubber cement (dotted line) over *outside* of eggshell's open end (a). Place fabric circle *face up* on table and spread rubber cement (dotted line) in ½″-wide border around edge of hole (b).

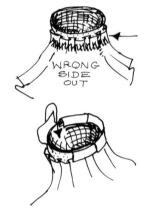

7. Holding eggshell *open end up*, fit hole in fabric *right side down* over it. Press glued surfaces together. *Note:* If fabric hole is too large for egg, overlap fabric edges slightly while glueing.

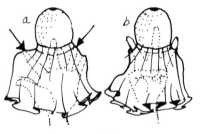

8. When fabric is firmly attached to egg, cut 1″-long strips of masking tape. Cover exposed rim of egg by pressing half of tape's width onto fabric and folding other half over (arrow) inside the egg, as shown. Add tape strips until rim is completely covered.

9. Turn egg *right side up*, folding back fabric. Place your middle finger inside egg and, with felt pen, mark fabric where index and ring fingers reach when comfortably spread (a). At marked points, cut holes large enough for fingers to stick out. These are puppet's arms (b).

10. Spread rubber cement over top of eggshell and press on wool "hair" (curls or short straight strands).

11. With pen or tempera paint, draw puppet's face.

(148)

April Fool's Day

Though April 1 has long been celebrated as a festival of spring, the origin of the custom of fooling people on this day is uncertain. It may be a relic of the ancient Roman feast in honor of Ceres, whose daughter, Proserpine, was carried off by Pluto, King of the Underworld, and made his Queen. Ceres' search for her daughter was considered a "fool's errand." Or perhaps the custom began in Northern and Central India, where a gay spring festival called *Huli* or *Holi* is celebrated at the end of March. People are sent on foolish errands, and men, women, and children join in the festivities by throwing or squirting colored powder or colored water on one another. Sweets are exchanged, and groups gather in the street to sing and dance.

Another theory explains that our modern April Fool tradition comes from France. Until fairly recent times, many countries celebrated their New Year at the end of March, near the time of the spring equinox (see *New Year*, page 92). It was not until 1582, when Pope Gregory XIII devised a new calendar, that the date of the new year was permanently changed to January 1. France was one of the first countries to adopt the new "Gregorian" calendar in the sixteenth century. News traveled slowly in those days, and many people, either because they did not know of the changed date or because they did not want to accept it, continued to celebrate on the old date, giving gifts and wishing each other a "Happy New Year" in the spring. Those who insisted upon observing in the old manner came to be known as "April Fools," or in French, *Poisson d'Avril* (pwah-sohn′ dahv-reel′), meaning "April Fish." French children receive chocolate fish on this day, and they play jokes on one another as we do in the United States.

POISSON d'AVRIL *(April Fish)*

For your April Fool's Day party, use the same fish motif for your invitations and for cupcake or cake decorations.

ERASER OR POTATO PRINT FISH

The fish design may be cut out of either one half of a potato or an art gum (soap) eraser. Unlike the potato, the eraser will not dry out and spoil, so the design is permanent unless broken or scratched. In either case, you will make a "relief" print. That is, everything that is raised, or in relief, will print, what is cut away will not.

Materials: Art gum eraser (3″ by 2″) or half potato, exacto knife or sharp block printing tool, tempera paint, brush, paper for card, tracing paper, ready-made envelopes large enough to fit card, newspaper to cover table.

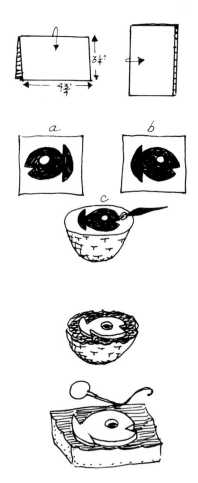

1. Decide shape of card, cut and fold paper. (In examples, paper is cut 6½″ by 4¾″ and folded to make card 3¾″ by 4¾″.)

2. Sketch fish on tracing paper (a). Turn paper face down; you are looking at reverse of sketched image (b). With tempera and brush, sketch this fish, as it appears *backwards*, on surface of potato (that has been blotted dry) or eraser (c). Fish will print in the *original* direction. *Note:* Fill in with paint the area you want to leave raised, which will print. Blank portions will be cut away.

3. Cover table with newspapers. With exacto knife (which is sharp and should not be used without permission or adult supervision) or block printing tool, cut around outline of fish, then cut away all blank areas. *Note:* ALWAYS CUT AWAY FROM HAND HOLDING ERASER OR POTATO, so if tool slips you will not be hurt. Brush away eraser or potato crumbs.

4. Keep tempera paint as thick as possible, so print will not be blurred. Brush thick paint over raised surface of eraser or potato (a). Place folded card *front side up* on newspaper-covered table. Turn eraser or potato *paint side down* and press onto card front. Press down hard, but do not slide design (b). Lift potato or eraser straight up off card and you have your print (c). Add invitation details with pen.

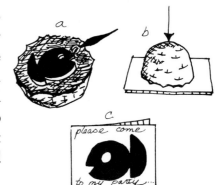

CAKE OR CUPCAKE STENCIL

Materials: Confectioners' sugar, sifter, tracing or typing paper that you can see through slightly, scissors, cake or cupcakes.

1. Sketch fish design in center of piece of paper which is slightly larger than entire surface of cake or cupcake. Design must be placed on paper in such a way that when design is centered on cake, the remaining surface of cake is covered with paper. *Note:* Omit fish's eye.

2. Cut out fish, making stencil, or hole in otherwise uncut paper.

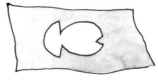

3. Center stencil on unfrosted cake or cupcake (or on a hard-glazed frosting which will not stick to paper). Pour about ½ cup of confectioners' sugar into sifter and sift over opening in stencil. Sugar will fall on paper as well as into hole; *do not move paper while sifting sugar or design will blur.*

4. When sugar has thoroughly coated fish stencil, lift paper *straight up above cake,* taking care not to spill any sugar, then move paper to side, away from cake top.

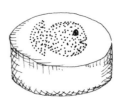

5. Jelly bean or other candy may be set in place for fish's eye.

(151)

In England, April 1 was commonly observed as a spring holiday, but the custom of fooling did not become popular until after the Gregorian calendar was accepted in 1752 and the New Year's date changed to January. English joke-playing is often limited to the morning hours, and if someone tries to trick you after noon, you can say, as they do in Hampshire, "April Fool's gone past; you're the biggest fool at last." To stop someone from playing a joke, you can say "pinch punch, first of the month, no returns of any kind." In Scotland, a favorite joke is to send someone out to hunt for a *gowk*, or cuckoo, and April Fools are also called "April Gowks."

GOWK HUNT

This is a good creative game for everyone to play at your April 1st party.

Materials: Scissors, pencils, crayons, drawing paper, tempera paints and brushes or colored felt pens, large paper bag or box, assorted collage materials (on separate table; colored papers, rubber cement, buttons, ribbons, wood scraps, stick, string, etc.), stiff paper such as bristol board or shirt cardboards for collage backing, prizes.

1. Give guests crayons and drawing paper and ask them each to draw an imaginary animal or bird. Then ask them to make up imaginary names for their creatures and write these names under the pictures.

2. Place all pictures into bag or box, and shuffle.

3. Pass around bag or box of pictures and have each guest draw one at random (while looking away as he chooses). If one draws his own picture, it should be replaced, the pictures shuffled, and drawn again.

4. Guests then go on a Gowk Hunt. If they don't think they can find an animal resembling the one they have selected—in say, five minutes, from their immediate surroundings—then they must make one as like it as possible in collage form by choosing materials from "collage table" and glueing them onto stiff paper or cardboard backing. Crayons and paints may also be used.

5. Have an exhibition of all finished collages hung beside the drawings which inspired them. Give prizes for the most original creature in first series of drawings (step 1), the best collage (step 4), or the funniest, etc.

Tango-no-Sekku

May 5 is the Japanese Boys' Festival, *Tango-no-Sekku* (tahn-goh-noh-sek-koo). Observed on the fifth day of the fifth month, it is also known as the "Feast of the Flags" and the "Kite Festival." The main activity of this day is the flying of kites, especially carp kites. Swimming upstream each year against the current to lay its eggs, this fish is an important symbol, for it represents perseverence, strength, and bravery—all qualities young boys hope to achieve. Made of paper or cloth, the kites, or banners, are also hung on poles outside boys' homes. Before some homes, there will be a carp for each son, the largest for the oldest.

CARP KITE

Materials: Colored or white tissue paper (usually comes in sheets 20″ by 29¾″), a strip of oaktag or 1-ply bristol board, tempera paint and brush or colored felt pens, old newspaper, rubber cement, darning needle, carpet thread, ruler, pencil, scissors.

1. Spread one sheet of tissue paper lengthwise on table and copy carp body shape at right along paper's diagonal. *Note:* The dotted lines dividing paper into quarters are included only as a guide to help you copy the pattern shapes. The body is *basically an oval,* and measures 31″ (in example) from mouth to tail and 9″ across widest part of belly. Mouth, *which must curve outward as shown for the last 2″,* is 6½″ wide at the end. Carp may be made any size as long as basic pattern shapes remain the same.

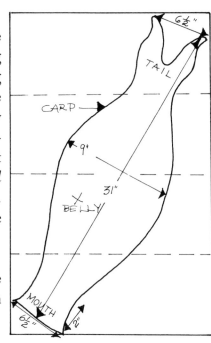

2. After drawing carp, turn paper over and make light pencil X on back of carp's belly. Then turn paper right side up again.

(153)

3. In the space around carp body, draw shapes A, B, and C as shown. A is back fin, measuring 7″ long, 2″ wide at peak. Fins B and C are both 4″ long, 2½″ wide at bottom, and taper to 1½″ at top.

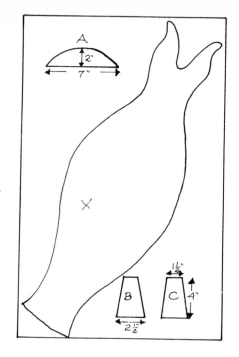

4. After drawing all shapes on first piece of tissue, place a second sheet of tissue on top of it, line edges up evenly, and tape corners. Then with pencil, trace over the carp body and fins B and C (*do not trace over shape A*) which show through from underneath. Make a light pencil X on *front* of second carp's belly as shown. Cut all shapes out of both pieces of tissue paper.

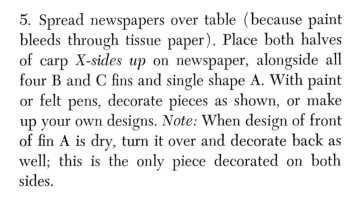

5. Spread newspapers over table (because paint bleeds through tissue paper). Place both halves of carp *X-sides up* on newspaper, alongside all four B and C fins and single shape A. With paint or felt pens, decorate pieces as shown, or make up your own designs. *Note:* When design of front of fin A is dry, turn it over and decorate back as well; this is the only piece decorated on both sides.

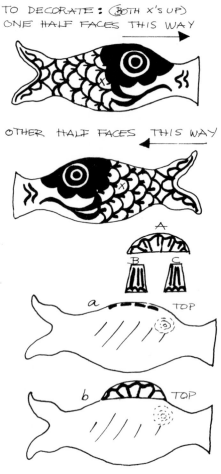

6. When designs are dry, place one half of carp body *decorated side down* on table. Spread ½″-wide border of rubber cement onto center of *top edge*, as shown (dotted lines, (a)). Press flat edge of fin A onto glue as shown, so curved top sticks up above carp's back (b).

(154)

7. Spread ½″ wide border of glue (dotted line) along top edge of body. Spread glue right over bottom of fin A (a). *Note: Do not spread glue on ends of tail or ends of mouth.* With *decorated side up*, press second carp over the first, pressing along glued top border. Fin A is now sandwiched between two halves of carp. Lift top carp, spread glue along bottom edge (b) of *bottom* carp (not on tail or mouth), and press sides together.

8. Turn four fins B and C *decorated sides down* on table. Spread ½″-wide strip of glue across narrow (top) end of each fin. Place carp flat on table and press glued ends of *two* fins in place as shown, one just behind gills, one just in front of tail. Turn carp over and glue two remaining fins in place.

9. Cut strip of oaktag or bristol board 12″ long, ⅜″ wide. To glue mouth into a ring, place carp flat on table as shown. Spread apart ends of mouth and brush *1″-wide* strip of glue (dotted lines) across inside of bottom half (a). Press strip onto glue, leaving ½″ of strip sticking out over *top* edge of mouth (arrow, (b)). Fold glued tissue edge over onto strip, covering it (c).

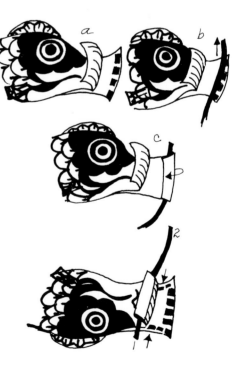

10. Turn carp over so covered strip is on top. Gently bend strip back as shown. Spread *1″-wide* border of glue (dotted lines) across inside of bottom half of mouth. Also spread ½″-wide border of glue along each side of mouth (arrows) until you reach previously joined edges (step 7).

(155)

11. Pinch together glued top *sides* of mouth as shown. (Bottom sides are joined in following step.) Bend loose end (2) of strip down as far as it will easily reach, so top edges of mouth meet. Press strip flat onto glued bottom as shown (a). Then bend short strip end (1) up and glue it flat, slightly overlapping end 2. This will make a ring in the mouth (b). Fold glued mouth bottom over onto strip, completely covering it. Pinch bottom sides of mouth (arrows) together, overlapping the tissue edges and glueing them to covered ring. Mouth should now be an opened, completely covered ring (c).

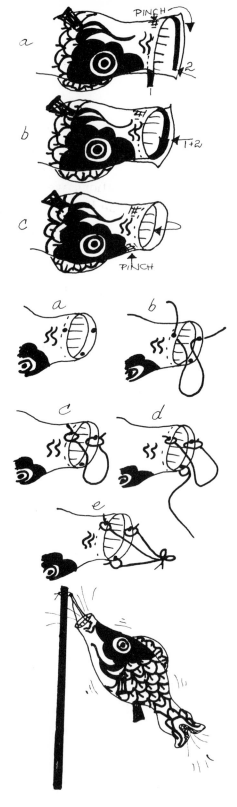

12. With pencil, mark three evenly spaced dots on mouth ring (a). Thread darning needle with piece of carpet thread 12″ long. Stitch into one mark and, holding one end of the thread in this hole, stitch across carp's mouth and out one of remaining holes. Remove needle (b). Tie each end of the thread to the ring in a double knot. Try to keep ends of knot short, in order to leave long piece of thread curving up in loop as shown (c). Thread darning needle with 7″-long thread and stitch through remaining hole. Remove needle, tie one end of thread to ring in a double knot (d). Pinch looped thread in half and tie remaining end of single thread to center in double knot as shown (e). *Note:* Keep all three legs same length.

13. Tie thread loop onto a stick, pole, or tree outside and carp will fill with wind.

May Day

The ancient Romans celebrated a feast called Floralia for six days at the end of April and the beginning of May in honor of the Goddess of Flowering Plants, Flora. They also honored the Goddess Maia, on the first day of her month, May. Decorations were made of branches of fruit and flowers, and Roman children made little flower dolls, called floras. Men sent branches, or sometimes whole trees, to the homes of their sweethearts.

FLORA DOLL

Materials: Flowers (one with long stem and fully opened head, a daisy is especially easy to work with), five or six (or more) other blooms, not necessarily fully opened, with long stems, two flower buds—each on long stem (optional), thin (#32) wire or carpet thread, scissors, stick (pencil-thick, as tall as you wish doll to be), straight pins or colored felt pen.

1. To make doll's head, place fully opened flower head against top of stick as shown, with stem running down the front of stick. To hold flower in this position, wind wire several times around stem and stick just under flower head.

2. If you have two buds, place one stem on each side of stick front and bend buds down as shown forming arms and hands, and wire base of stems onto stick.

3. To make skirt: Gather remaining flowers so their heads are approximately even with each other. Turn them upside down (a), and place them against front of stick. Wire these stems to stick a little below head of flower, making a "waist" (b). To make arms, if you have *not* used

a

b

(157)

buds, bend one of these stems down on each side of stick as shown (c). *Being careful not to damage head flower,* cut off all skirt stems just above point where they were wired (just under the head) Leave two arm stems sticking out (d).

4. With felt pen, draw face (dotted forms are the easiest to make), on center of head flower or stick straight pins into flower center to mark features.

When the Roman Empire spread to Northern Europe, it naturally took along its holidays, including the Floralia, which gradually developed into the elaborate occasion we know as May Day. Many of the earliest customs still survive. In England, for example, May Day morning is the time for young people to go "a-maying." Groups go into the country to gather hawthorn branches, greens, flowers, and sometimes whole trees for a maypole. Often they return with wreaths of flowers in their hair, and carrying long chains of woven flowers. Young girls also wash their faces in hawthorn dew on May Day morning to insure a good complexion, just as English girls have done for centuries. In Greece, wild flowers are gathered and woven into May Day wreaths. In some Greek villages, the wreaths are hung to dry until St. John's Eve, June 23, when they are burned in bonfires (see *Midsummer Day,* page 179).

The maypole is related to the ancient Roman tree-giving custom, though in Sweden, it is believed that the word "may" in "maypole" comes not from the month, but from the Old Swedish word *majar* (may-ar) meaning "to adorn with leaves or branches." The maypole is a nearly universal custom, the symbol of a living tree in which the spirit of growth awakens in the spring. In some European villages, the maypole is permanently fixed on the village green and left standing throughout the year. In other places, new poles are erected every year or every two years. In the village of Lanreath, in Cornwall, England, there is a custom called "Defense of the Maypole." The maypole must be guarded day and night during the entire week it is in place. Guards try to

(158)

protect the pole from the young people of neighboring villages who try to capture it. Maypoles may be of any size or height. Throughout Europe, they are commonly decorated at the top with garlands of flowers or ornaments. In some places a doll, or flower doll, sits at the top. The shaft is sometimes painted with stripes, but more often, it is left plain, with ribbon streamers hanging down to be wound around by the May Day dancers. In certain villages of Switzerland, it is the custom on *Maitag Vorabend* (may-tahg for-ah'-bind) or May Day Eve (April 30), for young men to decorate small pine trees with flowers and ribbons and place them beside the door of their girl friend's home, just as the ancient Roman boys did. An attractive girl might wake on May Day morning to find one, or even several, decorated trees. But the poor unpopular girl might find instead an ugly straw doll.

In memory, though long forgotten, of the ancient goddesses Flora and Maia, a May Queen is traditionally chosen from the girls of the town. In England, the May Queen wears a crown of forget-me-nots, and is crowned by the last year's Queen. The new monarch is led, children scattering rose petals in her path, in a grand procession across the village green to the "throne." This procession can be an elaborate affair, often led by the Town Crier ringing a bell. He is followed by the Queen, who usually has a May King, their court, and costumed villagers. Besides shepherds, shepherdesses, and milkmaids, the costumes might include jesters, chimney sweeps, Morris-dancers, and most important, Jack-in-the-green, or Robin Hood, and Maid Marian, Friar Tuck, and Little John. Robin Hood as we know him is a modern addition. Originally, he was a mythical figure of spring, called the "green man," or "Robin-of-the-wood," or "Jack-in-the-green"; he symbolized the spirit of seasonal growth. Maid Marian was originally a similar spirit of growth and fertility, the "May Queen" or "Maid May."

After the procession, the May Queen is installed in her throne and, with her court, she watches as dancers plait the maypole ribbons. The maypole dance is a "country dance" which may take many forms and be performed by both boys and girls. Often the traditional English Morris-dances are also performed. This type of folk dance is done only by male dancers, whose costume consists of a hat decorated with ribbons and flowers, streamers at wrist and elbow, and bells strapped around their shins and pinned to leg ribbons. White handkerchiefs are held in the hand, and wooden sticks are clacked. Originally, the bells and sticks were believed to frighten away the evil spirits, and the dancers' high leaps were to encourage the crops to grow tall. After the dances there are games on the village green such as hoop rolling and, because Robin Hood was a famous archer, archery.

FLOWER TOSS

As a substitute for archery, this "aim" game may be played at any spring party.

Materials: Seven empty, clean tuna fish cans (or other cans of similar size) with tops removed, 12 paper clips, dried beans or pebbles.

1. If desired, six of the cans may be decorated by glueing strips of colored or decorated paper around outside.

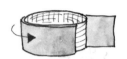

2. Arrange the empty cans as shown, with the undecorated one in the center, and the six others surrounding it. Paper clip cans together with their edges touching (dots).

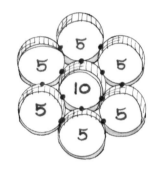

3. *Carefully* lift can "flower" and place it on ground or floor whatever distance you decide it should be behind a marked "throwing line."

4. Each player in turn takes 5 beans or pebbles and tosses them into the flower. Beans which land in *center* are worth *10 points*, beans which land in "*petals*" are worth *5 points*. Highest score wins.

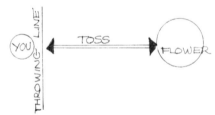

An unusual May Day custom is observed in Sweden, where country people sprinkle grass on their doorsteps. It is believed that this will keep away the witches who ride this night, for they will stop to count each blade of grass before entering the house, and by the time they have finished if it is not already dawn, at least those inside will be warned. In France, friends give each other lilies of the valley, called *muguets des bois* (mu-gay day bwah). The streets of Paris on May Day morning are full of country people who have come into the city at dawn carrying great baskets of muguets which they sell in small bouquets. It is said that if you make a wish while wearing muguets des bois given to you by someone you love, your wish will come true.

MUGUETS DES BOIS (*Lilies of the Valley*)

Materials: Scissors and sharp-pointed manicure scissors, white facial tissue, clean, empty tuna fish can (or similar size can), masking tape or florists' tape, cellophane tape, old newspapers, darning needle, thin (#32) wire, rubber cement and Elmer's or Sobo glue, water, wax paper, paper towel, green colored paper, pencil with new (unworn) eraser on end, corsage pin or straight pin.

1. Cover table with newspapers. Cut about nine 2″ squares of tissue. Mix glue with water in can until it is the consistency of thick cream. Dip the tissues one at a time into glue. Remove, keeping tissues as flat as possible and mold about ½″ down over end of pencil eraser. Cover cracks or lumps in molded tissue with another layer, so molded form finally is smooth and opaque. *Note:* Each blossom uses one or two tissues.

2. To remove excess glue from molded tissue, roll end of pencil gently over double layer of paper toweling. This will also help form tissue to eraser's shape.

3. *Gently* twisting molded tissue, slip it off end of pencil. *Do not squeeze it closed.* Set molded blossom gently on clean piece of wax paper until dry and hard (may take three hours or more). Repeat steps 1, 2, and 3 making three or more blossoms (cutting more squares of tissue as needed).

4. When blossoms are dry, poke a hole in center bottom of each with darning needle (a). With manicure scissors, cut out tiny wedges from around edge of each blossom top to make petals (b).

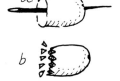

5. Cut one piece of wire 5″ long for main stalk, and several 3″-long pieces to attach blossoms to stalk. Make looped knot in one end of longest (stalk) wire (a). Stick this wire, *unknotted end*

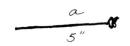

first, into one blossom. Pull wire end out as shown (b). Stick a pencil, eraser down, inside blossom to hold wire knot firmly on inside while you twist wire just beneath blossom into a small loop (c). This loop will keep blossom from sliding down wire. Repeat steps (a), (b), and (c) to attach all blossoms.

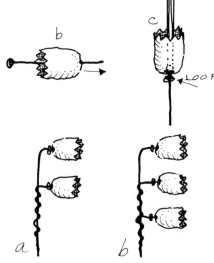

6. Bend over head of first blossom on stalk as shown. Just below it, wind on wire stem of another blossom. Twist this second wire tightly around full length of main stem (a). Add other blossoms to main stalk in the same manner (b). Line up blossoms along *same side* of main stalk.

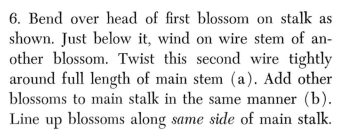

7. Wind stem wires from bottom up to just beneath last blossom with masking or florists' tape.

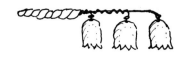

8. Trace and transfer (see page 18) or copy leaf pattern from page 132. Cut leaf out. Draw rib lines on front and back of leaf.

9. Spread rubber cement over base of leaf (X's). Spread rubber cement over tape on base of wire stems. Wrap base of stems in glued base of leaf.

10. Wind base of corsage with short length of florists' or cellophane tape to hold. Insert corsage or straight pin and wear your muguets on May Day.

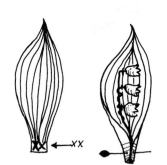

While May Day is considered to be primarily a festival welcoming spring, it has another, political, significance. In 1889, at an international meeting of Socialists, it was decided that May Day should be renamed "Labor Day," and made a holiday honoring the working man. Since that time, all countries with Socialist or Communist forms of government celebrate May 1 as Labor Day, with speeches and military parades.

(162)

Easter

To find the origin of the spring festival of Easter, one must go back to earliest history. Some authorities believe the tribes of northern and central Europe held their spring celebration in honor of the goddess Oestre, or Ostera (in Scandinavia, Ostra), whose Anglo-Saxon name was Eostre. Here name is also related to early forms of the word "east," showing that she was also the "dawn" goddess, as the sun rises in the east. Seeing the warmth of the sun return, the pagans gave thanks, offering their goddess sacramental cakes. Another interpretation explains that Oster, or Eostur, was the name of the ancient Norsemen's "season of the rising sun," or spring. From *Eostre* or *Eostur* comes, of course, our word "Easter." As the sun is "born" in the east, it is thought that "Easter" was originally a festival of the returning, "reborn" spring sun. With the arrival of Christianity, the sun's symbolism was transferred to Christ, who was "reborn" on Easter.

Christianity teaches that in the spring Christ was crucified, and after three days in the tomb, arose from the dead. The celebration of his resurrection quite naturally blended with, and finally absorbed, the early pagan festivals of nature's rebirth. Many modern Easter customs thus find their origin in pagan times. The sacramental cakes offered to the pagan goddess evolved into different types of Easter cakes, from the Portuguese *folar*, decorated with hard-boiled eggs, to the Russian "spring cakes," and our "hot cross buns" decorated with a sugar cross.

The custom of wearing flowered bonnets and new clothes in Easter parades began with the ancient belief that the earth put on new garments in the spring. It was therefore good luck to wear new clothes at the spring holiday.

The egg has always been a symbol of new life; some of the earliest men believed the world was hatched by the creator from an enormous egg. As a symbol, the egg has always been an important part of men's festivals. Since ancient times, the Jewish people have had a *paschal* egg, symbolizing new life, at their Passover feast (see page 171). In the spring, the ancient Romans honored the mythological twins Castor and Pollux, who were born from an egg of Leda, the swan. Their festival included races run in egg-shaped tracks and eggs given as prizes and gifts. Christians have long used the egg as the symbol of Christ's rebirth. Today in Italy, for example, on Easter, children are given gaily decorated egg-shaped candies; eggs are also taken to church for the priest's blessing, then honored in the home at the Easter feast. In the United States, eggs are dyed and decorated, and egg-rolling and egg-gathering contests are popular. One might push the egg along the grass with one's nose, balance the egg on a spoon while running, or win a prize for finding the greatest number of hidden eggs. On Easter Monday, there is a famous egg-rolling contest on the lawn of the White House in Washington, D.C. In Europe, egg-rolling games have long been popular. For example, in France during the eighteenth century, egg-rolling races were the main events of the Easter celebration, and great hogsheads of cider were given as prizes to the winners.

Easter eggs are dyed in almost every country. Red is the most popular color, one explanation for this being that eggs were dyed red in early Christian times in memory of the blood Christ shed during his crucifixion. In Greece, where the Eastern Orthodox Church usually celebrates Easter slightly later than the Roman Church, red is the traditional egg color. Eggs are generally dyed on Maundy Thursday, which for this reason is sometimes called "Red Thursday." After the midnight church service on Easter Sunday, the family returns home to the Easter feast. Red eggs are the first foods on the table, and after the feast, the following egg game is played.

THE KNOCKING OF THE EGGS AT EASTER

Materials: Hard-boiled eggs dyed red, prize for winner (optional).

Two players face each other, each holding a red, hard-boiled egg with the pointed tip up. Each tries to break the other's egg by knocking it with his own. The winner gains good luck and the broken egg of his opponent. Bets are often taken on whose egg will crack first, and cheaters have been known to try to slip in a wooden egg.

In the United States, as in Austria and Germany, children are told that the Easter rabbit brings the colored eggs. The rabbit is a symbol which, like the egg, had its origin in ancient times. In nearly every land, the rabbit, or hare, represents fertility and life. In addition, the hare is often associated wth the new moon. In modern China and Japan, even as in ancient Egypt, the hare is the symbol of the new moon, bringing a new life cycle for nature and for men.

The importance of the moon is further seen in the fact that it determines the date of the Easter holiday. Easter falls on the first Sunday after the first full moon after the spring equinox, the twenty-first of March. Thus, the date of Easter changes each year, falling sometime between March 22 and April 25. The official Easter season is preceded by the pre-Lenten carnival or "Mardi Gras" celebrations (see page 138), which end on Shrove Tuesday, the last care-free day before Ash Wednesday when Lent begins. The word "Lent" comes from the Old English *leinte* and *lencten* meaning "spring." The Lenten period includes the forty days before Easter. It is a solemn time in which Christians are supposed to deny themselves pleasures in memory of the forty days Jesus spent praying and wandering in the wilderness without food. Maundy Thursday, the Thursday of the Lord's Supper, is the day when Christ and his disciples celebrated the Last Supper, a Jewish Passover seder (see page 171).

Boys and girls in France, Italy, and many other Catholic European countries, believe that the Easter *bells*, not the Easter rabbit, bring their colored eggs. After Mass on Maundy Thursday, all the church bells are silent. The story is told that the bells have flown off to Rome to visit the Pope, to be blessed by him, and to sleep on the roof of St. Peter's Cathedral. While there, they will fetch the eggs to drop, when they return, into the houses and gardens of all good children. From Maundy Thursday through Good Friday, the day Christ was crucified, to Easter Sunday, when he arose, the church bells are silent. On Easter Sunday, all the bells joyfully ring out; Christ has risen, the bells have returned from Rome, and the children happily find their eggs.

Men have always loved the colors in nature and sought ways to copy them by making their own dyes. From fruits, flowers, and minerals in the earth, they made coloring for their wool, their cloth, their straw, and even for their makeup and hair. American Indians, particularly noted for their beautiful natural dyes, used vegetables, roots, walnuts, and tree bark among other things. The fabric dyes, vegetable food colorings, and egg dyes one finds today in markets are a recent innovation. These bright colors are very different from the softer, natural colors. Today, in countries where dyes cannot easily be bought, people still make their own, using vegetables and flowers just as their ancestors did. In the villages of Poland, for example, Easter eggs are colored with several natural materials. Some, like the brown made from walnuts, are difficult for us to duplicate because the boiled walnut husks and leaves are often hard to obtain and badly stain one's hands. Onion skins and saffron dyes are easier for us to make, and give soft green, yellow, and peach colors.

NATURAL EASTER EGG DYES

Materials: Red Spanish onions, yellow onions, saffron (the dry stigmas of a variety of crocus plant, used since ancient times as a yellow dye and food seasoning), white blown eggs (see page 147, step 1), saucepan, water, strainer, spoon, cups, paper towel, vinegar. *Note:* When experimenting with dyes, it is safer to blow the eggs rather than hard-boil them. Rub dyed eggs with bacon fat to shine, as is done in many European countries.

GREEN DYE

1. Peel dry outer skin from several red Spanish onions. The more skins used, the darker the dye. Place skins in about 2 cups water in saucepan and boil gently about 5 minutes. Stir occasionally.

2. Strain dye into a cup or small bowl and throw away skins. Add 1 tablespoon vinegar to dye. Set clean blown egg in dye. Turn egg occasionally, and leave in dye until color is as dark as you want it. Although this dye will appear reddish, the egg will become a soft olive green.

PEACH DYE

Repeat above steps 1 and 2 using dry outer skins of several yellow onions. Egg will turn a soft peach color.

YELLOW DYE

1. Place 5 or 6 (or more) pieces of saffron in saucepan with about 2 cups of water. Boil gently for about 5 minutes.

2. Strain dye into a cup, throw saffron away. Add 1 tablespoon vinegar. Place egg in dye, turn occasionally, and leave in dye until color is as dark as you want it. Egg will turn a soft yellow.

Originally a decorative art of the Easter season, the Polish *Wycinanka Ludowa* (vee-tchee-nan'-kah loo-doh'-vah), "folk paper cutout," is one of the most original and imaginative forms of folk art in the world. While the technique—cutting folded paper into symmetrical designs—appears to be simple, it is often developed into designs of great complexity. This unique art form developed its great popularity around the first half of the nineteenth century, with the Easter cock, or hen, as the main motif.

Today, designs are also made for Christmas and as year-round decorations. Though they are seen now in modern homes, the cut paper designs originally were, and often still are, pasted directly onto the whitewashed walls of the Polish peasant's home. They were kept on the wall from one Easter to the next; if they became too dusty in the living room, they were moved to the kitchen, and from there, if darkened by stove smoke, to the barn, for cows, too, like decorations on the holidays.

In addition to the traditional Easter cock, other motifs are the spruce tree, the human figure, village scenes, flowers, and stars. A glazed paper similar to Japanese origami paper is used, and the cutting is done with the same sharp pointed shears used for shearing sheep. The designs, when not mounted directly to the wall, are glued to flat white mounting paper or to the front of folded stiff paper for greeting cards. Cut-paper shapes may also be glued on to clean, blown Easter eggs.

WYCINANKA LUDOWA (*Polish Folk Paper Cutouts*)

The patterns on page 170 are adaptations of the traditional Easter "Cocks in a Tree" and "Tulip." Once you see how the designs are formed by cutting folded paper into basic shapes and then trimming with delicate fringe cuts, you may adapt the patterns to your own designs. The "Cocks in a Tree" are simply cut from one piece of folded paper, while the tulip is built up in several layers of differently shaped and colored papers. These shapes may be glued onto Easter, or other holiday cards, or scaled down into smaller sizes and glued onto blown, plain, or colored Easter eggs.

(167)

Materials: Thin colored paper such as glazed or origami paper, sharp-pointed manicure scissors or exacto knife (which is very sharp and should not be used without permission or adult supervision), old magazine (to cut on if using knife), rubber cement, card paper such as construction paper, tweezers, crayon or felt pen.

BASIC CARD

To make card, cut piece of construction paper 5″ by 9″. Fold in half lengthwise, as shown. Press along fold.

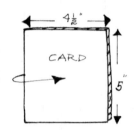

COCKS IN A TREE

1. Trace pattern A, page 170. Fold a piece of colored glazed or origami paper in half, making sure both halves are large enough for entire pattern. Place pattern's dotted line along the fold and transfer (see page 18) pattern to paper.

2. After transferring, hold both sides of folded paper firmly together and cut around outline of shape.

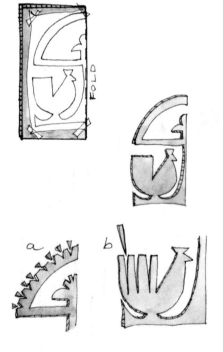

3. After basic shape is cut, fringe is added. Hold folded paper firmly together and, using points of scissors (or exacto knife on magazine) cut tiny narrow wedges in from the edges as shown (a) around outside of tree and around top of ball in tree's center. On bird's tails, cut longer, narrow wedges as shown (b).

4. Carefully open shape and press flat on table. Turn face down onto scrap paper and brush entire back with even layer of rubber cement (a). Lift shape up, using tweezers to pull up any bits of fringe that cling to scrap paper, and press de-

(168)

sign, glue side down, onto front of folded card (b). If any area does not stick, add a bit more glue. When glue is dry, carefully (so fringe does not tear) rub off excess glue. With crayon or felt pen, write greeting inside (or around design outside) card.

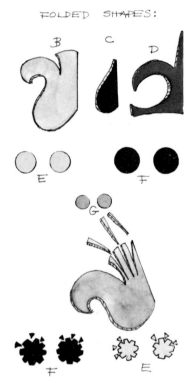

FOLDED SHAPES:

TULIP

1. Follow directions for Basic Card above.

2. Follow steps 1 and 2 above to trace, transfer and cut out patterns B, C, and D, page 170. *Note:* Shape B and C should be cut from differently colored paper.

3. Trace and transfer patterns E, F, and G. From folded or single-layer of paper, cut two shapes E (of a different color than D), two shapes F, and two shapes G (of a different color than F).

4. To cut fringe in the center of folded shape B, cut out 3 long narrow wedges with points of manicure scissors.

5. Cut tiny, narrow wedges in from edges of two shapes F and two shapes E. (Do not fold these shapes to cut fringe.)

6. Following directions in step 4 of *Cocks*, spread glue over backs of all shapes. To glue onto card, first place down stem shape D, then B above it and C over the center of B, as shown (a). Then press unfringed circles G in center of each flower F, and add plain star flowers E (b). With pen or crayon, add greeting.

(169)

A

B

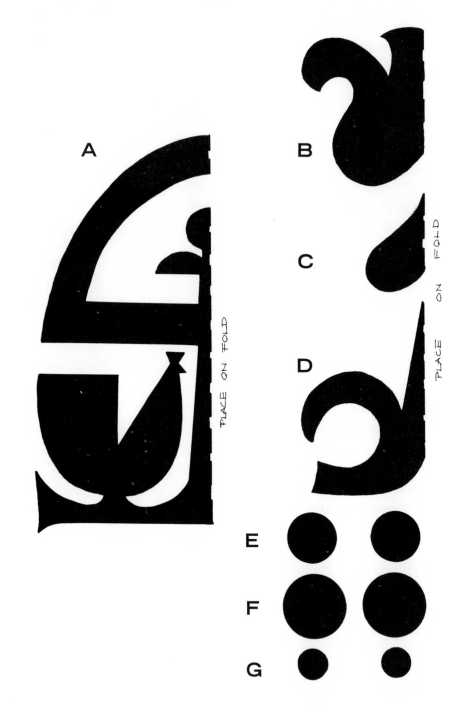

PLACE ON FOLD

C

PLACE ON FOLD

D

E

F

G

Passover

The spring celebration of *Passover,* one of the most important holidays of the Jewish religion, had its origin in earliest history. Canaan was the ancient name of the middle eastern region which later came to include Palestine and Syria. The people of this fertile area west of the Jordan River were primarily agricultural. To protect their crops of figs, grapes, wheat, and barley, they worshipped local gods called *baals,* and held seasonal rites to honor the sun, moon, and rain. Memories of these gods, known to the earliest wandering tribes, were thus carried into Egypt by Jacob and his twelve sons when they migrated from Canaan. The enslavement of the Hebrew tribes in Egypt is believed to have occurred under Pharaoh (King) Rameses II, who lived from 1299 to 1232 B.C. It was during the time when his successor, Merneptah, came into power that Moses led the Hebrew tribes out of slavery, out of Egypt. During the period of coming out, or "exodus," from Egypt, and through their later wanderings, these people chose one of the gods, Jehovah, as their own, the source of all their inspiration. With their migration into Palestine (at the time of the Iron Age, about 1200 B.C.), Jehovah replaced the local baals and became the God of Israel. His worship emphasized the idea of *one* god, and the elaborate temple ceremonies developed in his honor evolved into a new religion called Judaism, whose basic laws had already been set down by Moses when he received the Ten Commandments from God on Mount Sinai.

As the ancient agricultural festivals were adopted by the Hebrews, they were explained in terms of the new religion. The spring festivals of Pesach and Massôth, for example, were combined in the Jewish religion and given additional meaning in terms of the exodus from Egypt, which had occurred at the same time of the year, in the Hebrew month of Nisan (March–April). This is seen in the name of the early festival *Pesach,* which in Hebrew literally meant "skipping" or "gamboling"; after the exodus, the word was re-interpreted to mean the "skipping over" or "passing over" of Jewish homes by the Angel of Death. Thus today, *Pesach* means "Passover."

According to Jewish tradition, God sent two messengers, Moses and his brother Aaron, to beg the Egyptian Pharaoh to free the Hebrew people from slavery. He refused, and as punishment, God sent ten plagues down upon the Egyptians: water turned to blood; frogs; lice; wild beasts; cattle disease; skin disease; hail; locusts; and darkness. Though Egyptians (and Jews as well) suffered throughout these nine, Pharaoh would not soften. The tenth plague was the death of the firstborn male child in every family. For protection, the Jews smeared the blood of the lamb on their doorposts. Because of this sign, the Angel of Death "passed over" every Jewish home, killing only the Egyptian children. The Egyptians were stunned by their children's deaths, and as Pharaoh was himself a firstborn son, he was frightened for his life. He called for Moses and Aaron and ordered them immediately to lead the Jews out of Egypt. Every year since, Jewish people throughout the world have celebrated Passover as a festival of freedom, recalling their escape from slavery in Egypt.

Passover was traditionally observed for seven days, from the fifteenth to the twenty-first of Nisan. Today, only the Jews of Israel and Reform Jews of other countries celebrate it for seven days; Orthodox and Conservative Jews celebrate the festival for eight days, the first two being the most important. The primary activity of these first two evenings is a special feast called a *seder* (say'-der), meaning "order," because a particular order is followed. During the seder, the *haggadah* (hah-gad'-dah) or story of the exodus, is read. In stories, prayers, psalms, and songs, the haggadah explains the historical and religious meaning of the holiday. A special "seder plate" contains a roasted lamb bone and a roasted egg, symbolizing the ancient paschal sacrifices; *maror*, or bitter herbs (horse-radish) symbolizing the suffering of the Jews while slaves in Egypt; *charoseth* (hah-roh'-set), a mixture of wine, chopped apples, and nuts, representing the mortar which the enslaved Jews used to build for Pharaoh; salt water, symbolizing their tears while slaves; and *karpas*, a green vegetable symbolizing hope and new growth in the spring. The seder ends with the singing of such traditional songs as *Chad Gadya* (hah-god-yah), "An Only Kid." This is a folk song which tells of a father who bought a little goat, or kid, for two *zuzim*, ancient Hebrew coins. The kid is then eaten by a cat, who is bitten by a dog, who is beaten by a stick, etc., until finally God appears and restores order. One interpretation of this song tells that it is symbolic of early Jewish history: the kid is really the Jewish people; the man who bought it is God; the cat the Assyrians who took ten tribes of Israel into captivity; the dog, Babylonians; the stick, Persians; the water, Romans; the ox, the Saracen Empire; the butcher, the Crusaders; the Angel of Death, Turks; the Holy One, the Messiah. Some believe this song may have been the inspiration for the folk song and story *The House That Jack Built*.

It is interesting to remember that Christ was a Jew, and his Last Supper with his disciples in Jerusalem was a *Pesach*, or Passover, seder. The Early Christian idea of the "lamb of God" is thus derived from the traditional "paschal lamb." The name for Easter in many languages is also related to this Hebrew holiday: in Latin it is *Festa Paschalia;* in Italian, *Pasqua;* in French, *Pâques;* and in Spanish, *Pascuas*.

CHAD GADYA   (Music may be found in any haggadah in library or synagogue)

(1)

An only kid!
An only kid!
My father bought
For two zuzim.
An only kid! An only kid!

(2)

Then came the cat
And ate the kid
My father bought
For two zuzim.
An only kid! An only kid!

(3)

Then came the dog
And bit the cat,
That ate the kid
My father bought
For two zuzim.
An only kid! An only kid!

(4)

Then came the stick
And beat the dog,
That bit the cat,
That ate the kid
My father bought
For two zuzim.
An only kid! An only kid!

(5)

Then came the fire
And burned the stick,

That beat the dog,
That bit the cat,
That ate the kid
My father bought
For two zuzim.
An only kid! An only kid!

(6)

Then came the water
And quenched the fire,
That burned the stick,
That beat the dog,
That bit the cat,
That ate the kid
My father bought
For two zuzim.
An only kid! An only kid!

(7)

Then came the ox
And drank the water,
That quenched the fire,
That burned the stick,
That beat the dog,
That bit the cat,
That ate the kid
My father bought
For two zuzim.
An only kid! An only kid!

(8)

Then came the shohet*
And slaughtered the ox,
That drank the water,
That quenched the fire,
That burned the stick,

(* *shohet—ritual slaughterer*)

That beat the dog,
That bit the cat,
That ate the kid
My father bought
For two zuzim.
An only kid! An only kid!

(9)

Then came death's angel
And slew the shohet,
That slaughtered the ox,
That drank the water,
That quenched the fire,
That burned the stick,
That beat the dog,
That bit the cat,
That ate the kid
My father bought
For two zuzim.
An only kid! An only kid!

(10)

Then came the Holy One,
    praised be he,
And destroyed death's angel
That slew the shohet,
That slaughtered the ox,
That drank the water,
That quenched the fire,
That burned the stick,
That beat the dog,
That bit the cat,
That ate the kid
My father bought
For two zuzim.
An only kid! An only kid!

CHAD GADYA MOBILE

This mobile, consisting of all the figures from the traditional song, may be made before Passover begins and hung as a decoration throughout the holiday. During the seder, the mobile will help you remember the words of the song *Chad Gadya*.

Materials: Colored or white paper (such as construction paper), pencil, scissors, crayons or tempera paints and brush or colored felt pens, thin (#32) wire or carpet thread, darning needle, stiff but flexible wire (a clothes hanger will do nicely but you may need pliers or adult help in bending it), old newspapers, cup hook (or other hook in door sill or ceiling from which to hang mobile), masking tape.

1. Bend stiff wire into a circle about 12″ across.

2. Trace (or copy) heavy outlines of patterns on page 176–177, or make up your own designs. Transfer (see page 18) shapes to colored or white paper and cut them out. Spread newspaper over work area, color or paint details on one side of each shape as shown in patterns. When dry, turn shapes over and decorate other sides.

3. Cut three pieces of thin wire or carpet thread each 16″ long. Cut one piece 24″ long. At three points equal distances apart on wire ring, tie one end of each 16″ piece. Trim off short end of wire or thread after tying knot.

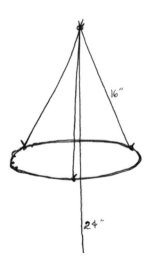

4. Gather the loose ends of these three wires (step 3). Between them, insert one end of the 24″-long wire as shown, so the other end hangs down inside ring. While holding the ends together, adjust the three shorter wires until they are of equal length and the ring hangs perfectly flat. Tie all four ends together.

(174)

5. Hang knotted ends from a hook, allowing central thread to hang down in center of ring. Slide the three knots along ring until they are equal distance apart and ring hangs flat. Spread a drop of rubber cement over each knot on ring to hold it in place.

6. To attach star, take point of scissors or pencil and poke small hole through X in top. Tie star onto wire hanging down in center of ring as shown. *Note:* Star should hang down about 3″ or 4″ below ring. Cut off extra thread after tying knot.

7. Thread darning needle with carpet thread or thin wire about 9″ long and stitch through top X of the other paper shapes. Remove needle and tie one end of the thread to itself over top of shape as shown, leaving the other end long to attach to mobile. Trim off extra thread hanging from knots.

8. To tie shapes onto ring: Begin with kid, attaching shapes (*three between each wire holding up ring*) in same order as they appear in song *Chad Gadya* (kid, cat, dog, stick, fire, water, ox, shohet, death's angel). Tie threads on ring with double knot, letting shapes hang down until they are about even with star. Trim off extra thread hanging from knots.

9. Slide knots holding shapes along ring until they are evenly spaced and ring hangs flat. Spread a drop of rubber cement over each knot on ring to hold it in place. Hang up mobile.

KID

CAT

FIRE

DOG

STICK

OX

WATER

SHOHET

STAR (HOLY ONE)

DEATH'S ANGEL

(177)

SUMMER

The longest day of the year is the summer solstice when, in the northern hemisphere, the sun reaches its highest point in the sky and is about to begin moving down toward the horizon again. Midsummer Day, the primary pagan summer festival, has always been observed near the date of the summer solstice, which usually occurs on June 21. Since ancient times, this day has been celebrated with fire ceremonies related to the pagan Celtic "beltane" fires of May (see page 142). To give the sun the strength and encouragement to remain rather than sink lower in the sky, bonfires were lit. Flaming torches were carried in processions and flaming cartwheels were rolled down hills. The fires were also believed to protect people from witches and evil spirits who were especially active on this day. Because of the nearness of these "spirits," Midsummer Day was, and often still is, considered a good time for luck or love charms and potions. Most of the Midsummer customs observed today had their origin in these ancient beliefs.

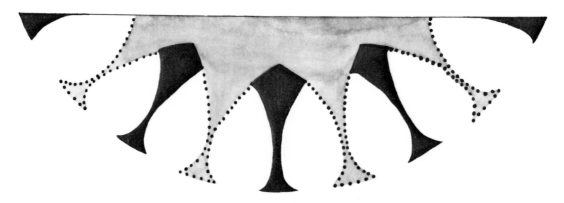

Midsummer Day, St. John's Day

Today in England, Midsummer Day is observed by the Companions of the Most Ancient Order of Druids, whose spiritual ancestors were the nature-worshipping Celtic tribes. Each year they hold a dawn ceremony at their traditional holy place, Stonehenge. Wearing white robes with scarlet hoods, they have a procession around the circle containing the altar stone while they salute the rising sun. In Cornwall, England, Midsummer bonfires form chains of light across the hilltops on the night of June 23. Flowers are thrown into the fires, and young couples jump over the flames hoping to insure their early marriages. In France, torches are carried and bonfires lit. Children jump over the flames in the ancient belief that crops will grow as high as one can jump. In Austria, too, boys carry flaming torches around bonfires while girls throw flowers into the flames. Here the farmers believe their hemp will grow as high as they can jump over the flames. In some villages, lovers jump over the flames holding hands, for then they can never be parted.

JUMP THE FLAME

Materials: Exacto knife, scissors, ruler, pencil, crayons or colored felt pens or tempera paint and brush, paper clamps (see page 15), masking tape, rubber cement, stiff (corrugated or mat) cardboard, prizes.

1. To make stand for flame, cut a piece of corrugated cardboard about 45″ long and 12″ wide. (If your cardboard is not long enough, tape *and* glue two overlapping pieces together.) Measure, mark, and draw a line across this strip 6″ up from one end. Then measure and draw lines across strip 13″ up from first line, then again, 13″ up from that, as shown, making four sections.

(179)

2. To make cardboard fold easily, the lines must be "scored." To do this, see page 19.

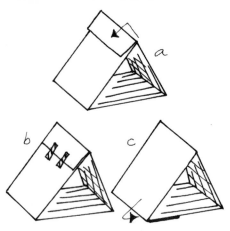

3. Turn scored cardboard over, *cut side* down. Fold up the three equal sections into a tepee. The short flap goes over outside of top, as shown (a). Spread rubber cement beneath this flap, then press it firmly down against side. Then tape outside of flap with masking tape, as shown (b). Finally, turn tepee over so flap is on *bottom*. Stand is now in correct position.

4. To make flames, cut three rectangles of stiff cardboard—one 12″ by 18″, one 12″ by 22″, one 12″ by 26″. Sketch, then cut each rectangle into flame shape, as shown. Try not to cut away too much height when shaping flame. Paint or crayon flame-colored designs on one side.

5. With paper clamps, fasten flame to one flat side of stand, as shown.

6. Beginning with shortest flame, the 18″, have each player in turn take a running start and jump over flame. Remove the 18″ flame and clamp on the 22″. All players who clear the 18″, then try to jump over the 22″ flame. Those who clear this go on to try the 26″ flame. Add taller flames if needed, or instead of making them, simply slide the tallest flame you have higher up along the stand as shown. Whoever jumps over the highest flame wins prize.

When Christianity spread throughout the pagan world, the Midsummer festival on June 24 was made the celebration of the birth of St. John the Baptist. Many of the pre-Christian Midsummer rites were given Christian symbolism. The traditional bonfires were renamed "St. John's Fires," and the day itself was called St. John's Day, because John was called a "burning light" by Christ. Herbs picked on this day were believed to have special healing powers, and in Germany, for example, they are called *Johanneskräuter* (yo-han'-nes-kroy'-ter), or St. John's herbs. In England, the herb St.-John's-wort is picked together with rue, trefoil, and vervain and they are tied into a "midsummer man" doll. (See *Flora Doll*, page 157.) In the Russian Ukraine, it is the custom in the country for girls and boys to dance around bonfires on St. John's Night, telling stories of magical ferns which mysteriously flower once a year, on this night. At midnight, they carry special potions into the woods searching for the fern flowers, which if found, bring good luck. Girls also make and wear flower wreaths, which, at the end of the holiday, they throw into a river.

In Germany, the sun's "falling" is celebrated on St. John's Day in some villages with burning wheels rolled down hills, symbolizing the sun's descent. Wooden wheels are usually used, wrapped with straw and set afire. It is good luck if your wheel burns all the way to the bottom of the hill.

FLAMING WHEEL CONTEST

This adaptation of the European flaming wheel races may be played by a whole group or by as few as two contestants.

Materials: "Hula" hoop or barrel hoop, red, orange, and yellow construction paper, masking or cellophane tape, pencil, scissors, prizes.

1. Cut red, orange, and yellow flame-shaped pieces of construction paper about 4″ long, tapering to a bottom width of about 1″ and at the top to a point, as shown. Cut as many shapes as you need to cover inside of hoop when they are placed side by side. See step 2.

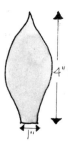

(181)

2. Tape bottom of each flame to *inside* of hoop, as shown (a). Press on strips of tape lengthwise, so they do not show on top surface of hoop (b). The completed hoop has rolling surface free of tape, and flames *all stick out on one side* leaving a clear edge for you to run beside.

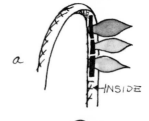

3. Each contestant, with hoop, lines up at starting line. When signal is given, they roll hoops toward finish line; track distance may be however long you wish. Whichever hoop reaches finish line first, having remained upright throughout the course, wins. Hoops which fall during race are disqualified. Winner receives prize.

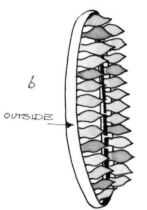

In South America, young girls observe many love superstitions on *El Día de San Juan* (el dee'-ah day sahn-hwan'), St. John's Day. Fortunes are told from the shapes made when melted lead is dripped into cold water. (This may be done more safely with wax, as described on page 29.) In Paraguay, crosses made of laurel leaves are placed under a girl's pillow so she will dream of her future husband.

In Sweden, the Midsummer celebration begins the evening before and continues throughout the day of June 24. It is a day of unusual festivities which center around a maypole, believed to take its name not from the month, but from the Old Swedish word *majar* (may-ar) meaning "to adorn with leaves or branches." The tall pole, usually a peeled spruce trunk, is covered with garlands of evergreens and birch leaves. Partway up, a crossbar carries several wreaths of wild flowers and greens, and a heart-shaped garland is attached to the pole as shown. The townspeople gather for the ceremony of the maypole raising. Fiddlers play folk melodies as parents, children, and grandparents join hands and dance around the pole. In many villages, national costumes are worn to these festivities.

(182)

In Finland, as in Sweden, young people dance around bonfires in their national costumes. Some of the most curious Midsummer rites of early pagan times were held in Finland, Sweden, and Lapland, where ancient maze sites have been discovered—some made of huge stones, others of pebbles. Stone mazes have also been found in the British Isles, but dating from a later period. The ancient mazes were part of the ritual worship of a king-god, perhaps the "sun," who was supposedly concealed in the center of the maze. In England, a form of maze ritual still exists, in a game played by school children called "Troy Town." Mazes are drawn and passed among the children as puzzles, though originally they were paths cut into the ground and marked with stones.

MAZES

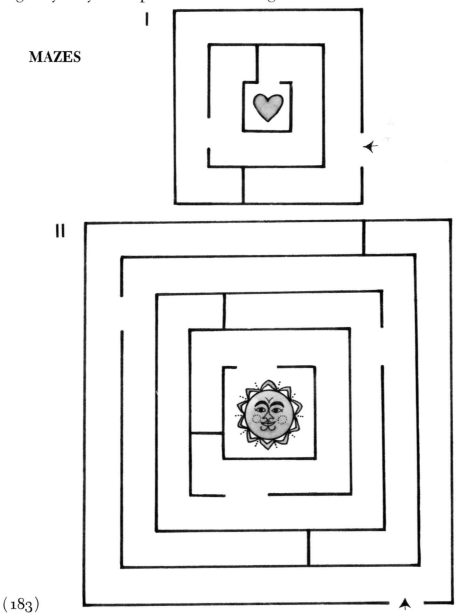

MAZES

Materials: Colored or white paper, crayons or felt pens.

1. First solve the easier maze I (page 183), then solve maze II. Beginning at the arrow, go in the "door," and with your finger (*do not write in the book*), trace along the inside of the hall until you reach the center heart and sun. If you come up against a blank wall, turn around and go back down the hall until you find an open "door" that leads you to another hall nearer the center.

2. a. To make your own maze, begin by drawing an object in maze center, such as a tree. Surround object with a wall, leaving one open space, or "door," as shown.

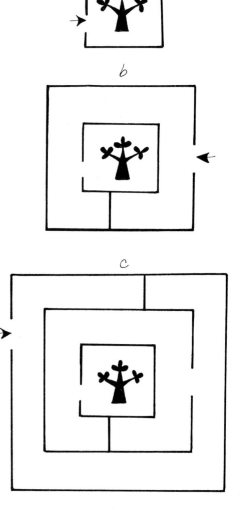

b. Draw a second wall around the first, leaving a hall between them. Leave an open "door" along this wall. At some point along the hall, not too close to the open "door," draw a line across connecting the two walls and making *one* "blank wall." This blank wall is a teaser, into which you will bump while trying to find the open path to the center.

c. Add a third wall, following step (b), leaving an open "door" and at one point drawing a blank wall across hall. Add as many outer walls as you wish. If desired, a prize may be given to member of group who solves maze in the quickest time, or who makes up the most difficult or unusual maze. For a beach party, guests may draw large mazes in the sand for each other to solve. Draw with sticks, placing seashells at center. If maze is large enough, hop along the halls (as in hopscotch) until you reach the center, pick up a shell, and hop out.

Activities Subject Index

The following subject index has been included as a guide to aid in the selection of activities. The projects are graded according to relative difficulty of execution: "1" refers to the simplest; "2" to those requiring more skill and time; and "3" to the most complicated.

(186)

Bibliography

Books and Periodicals

Achelis, Elisabeth. *Of Time and the Calendar.* New York: Hermitage House, 1955.

Bulfinch, Thomas. *The Age of Fable or Beauties of Mythology.* Boston: S. W. Tilton & Co., 1894.

Burke, Mrs. C., ed. *The Language of Flowers.* Los Angeles: Price, Stern, Sloan, Publishers, Inc., 1965.

Cagner, Ewert, ed. *Swedish Christmas.* New York: Henry Holt & Co., 1959.

Chambers, R., ed. *The Book of Days.* Vols. I, II. Philadelphia: Lippincott, 1863–64.

Deens, Edward M., ed. *Holy Days and Holidays.* New York: Funk & Wagnalls Co., 1902.

Dockstader, Frederick. *Indian Art in Middle America.* Greenwich, Conn.: N. Y. Graphic Society Publishers, Ltd., 1964.

Douglas, George William. *The American Book of Days.* New York: H. W. Wilson Company, 1948.

Eberhard, Wolfram. *Chinese Festivals.* New York: Henry Schuman, 1952.

Frazer, Sir James George. *The Golden Bough.* New York: The Macmillan Company, 1922.

Gaster, Theodor. *New Year: Its History, Customs and Superstitions.* New York: Abelard-Schuman, 1955.

Gaster, Theodor. *Purim and Hanukkah.* New York: Henry Schuman, 1950.

Grabowski, Jósef. *Wycinanka Ludowa.* Warszawa: Polska Sztuka, 1955.

Hamilton, Edith. *Mythology.* Boston: Little, Brown and Company, 1940.

Hottes, Alfred Carl. *1001 Christmas Facts and Fancies.* New York: Dodd, Mead & Co., 1946.

Ickis, Marguerite. *The Book of Festival Holidays.* New York: Dodd, Mead & Co., 1964.

Irwin, Keith Gordon. *The 365 Days.* New York: Thomas Y. Crowell Company, 1963.

James, E. O. *Seasonal Feasts and Festivals.* New York: Barnes & Noble, 1963.

Josephy, Alvin M., Jr., ed. *American Heritage Book of Indians.* New York: American Heritage Publishing Company, 1961.

Karpeles, Maud, and Blake, Lois. *Dances of England and Wales.* New York: Chanticleer Press, Inc., 1951.

Krythe, Maymie R. *All About American Holidays.* New York: Harper & Row, Publishers, 1962.

Lee, Ruth Webb. *A History of Valentines.* New York: Studio Publications, Inc., & Thomas Y. Crowell Company, 1952.

Lehner, E. & J. *Folklore and Symbolism of Flowers, Plants and Trees.* Tudor Publishing Co., 1960.

Linton, Adelin and Ralph. *Halloween Through Twenty Centuries.* New York: Henry Schuman, 1950.

Mexico This Month. Vol. XI, No. 6, Nov. 1965; Vol. XII, No. 7, Dec. 1966. Mexico, D.F.: Gráfica de Mexico, Publisher.

Meyer, Robert E., Jr. *Festivals Europe.* New York: Ives Washburn, Inc., 1954.

Opie, Iona, and Peter. *The Lore and Language of Schoolchildren.* Oxford: Clarendon Press, 1959.

Patten, Helen Philbrook. *The Year's Festivals.* Boston: Dana Estes & Co., 1903.

Simmons, Adelma. *A Book of Valentine Remembrances.* Coventry, Conn.: Caprilands Herb Farm.

Spence, Lewis. *Myths and Legends of Ancient Egypt.* London: George Harrap & Co., 1949.

Spence, Lewis. *Myth and Ritual in Dance, Game, and Rhyme.* London: Watts & Co., 1947.

Spicer, Dorothy Gladys. *Festivals of Western Europe.* New York: H. W. Wilson Co., 1958.

Toor, Frances. *Festivals and Folkways of Italy.* New York: Crown Publishers, Inc., 1953.

Walsh, William S. *Curiosities of Popular Customs.* Philadelphia: Lippincott, 1897.

Weiser, Francis X. *Handbook of Christian Feasts and Customs.* New York: Harcourt, Brace & Co., 1958.

Weiser, Francis X. *The Holyday Book.* New York: Harcourt, Brace & Co., 1956.

Wright, A. R. *British Calendar Customs, England.* London: Folklore Society, William Glaisher, Ltd., Vol. I, 1936; Vol. II, 1938.

Encyclopedias and Dictionaries

Dictionary of Catholic Biography. New York: Doubleday & Company, Inc., 1961.

Dictionary of Folklore, Mythology and Legend. Maria Leach, ed. New York: Funk & Wagnalls, 1950. Vols. I, II.

Encyclopedia Britannica, Inc. Chicago: William Benton, Publisher, 1960.

Larousse Encyclopedia of Mythology. New York: Prometheus Press, 1959.

New Catholic Encyclopedia. New York: McGraw-Hill Book Co., 1967.

New Jewish Encyclopedia. David Bridger & Samuel Wolk, New York: Behrman House, Inc., 1962.

Oxford English Dictionary. Oxford: Oxford University Press, 1933.

The Standard Jewish Encyclopedia. Cecil Roth, ed., New York: Doubleday & Co., Inc., 1966.

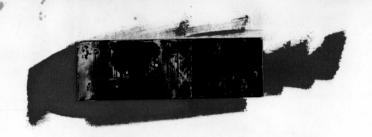